THE *secret* LIFE OF THE MORRIS MINOR

KAREN PENDER

VELOCE PUBLISHING PLC
PUBLISHERS OF FINE AUTOMOTIVE BOOKS

Dedication

To all Morris Minors everywhere - may your trunnions never wear out, nor your suspensions collapse!
To Richard for giving me support while I was carrying out the research for this book, and to Pepper the dog who created distractions and caused me to take much longer than I had originally intended to complete this work.

Other books of interest to enthusiasts available from Veloce -

Alfa Romeo, How to Power Tune Alfa Romeo Twin-Cam Engines (SpeedPro Series)
by Jim Kartalamakis
Alfa Romeo Giulia Coupé GT & GTA
by John Tipler
Alfa Romeo Modello 8C 2300
by Angela Cherrett
Alfa Romeo Owner's Bible
by Pat Braden
Biggles!
by Peter Berresford Ellis & Jennifer Schofield
Bubblecars & Microcars: Colour Family Album
by Andrea & David Sparrow
Big Bugattis - Types 46 & 50
by Barrie Price
Bugatti 57 - The Last French Bugatti
by Barrie Price
Bugatti Types 46 & 50
by Barrie Price
Car Bodywork & Interior: Care & Repair
by David Pollard
Citroën 2CV: Colour Family Album
by Andrea & David Sparrow
Citroën DS: Colour Family Album
by Andrea & David Sparrow
Cobra: The Real Thing!
by Trevor Legate
Completely Morgan: Three-Wheelers 1910-1952
by Ken Hill
Completely Morgan: Four-Wheelers 1936-1968
by Ken Hill
Completely Morgan: Four-Wheelers from 1968
by Ken Hill

Daimler SP250 'Dart'
by Brian Long
Fiat & Abarth 124 Spider & Coupé
by John Tipler
Fiat & Abarth 500 & 600
by Malcolm Bobbitt
Lola T70
by John Starkey
Making MGs
by John Price Williams
Mazda MX5/Miata Enthusiast's Workshop Manual
by Rod Grainger & Pete Shoemark
MGB, How to give your MGB V8 Power (SpeedPro Series)
by Roger Williams
Mini Cooper: The Real Thing!
by John Tipler
Motorcycling in the '50s
by Jeff Clew
Nuvolari: When Nuvolari Raced
by Valerio Moretti
Pass the MoT
by David Pollard
Porsche 911 R, RS & RSR
by John Starkey
Rover P4 Series (60•75•80•90•95•100•105•110)
by Malcolm Bobbitt
Triumph TR6
by William Kimberley
Vespa: Colour Family Album
by Andrea & David Sparrow
Volkswagen Karmann Ghia
by Malcolm Bobbitt

First published in 1995 by Veloce Publishing Plc., Godmanstone, Dorset DT2 7AE, England. Fax 01300 341065

ISBN 1 874105 55 3

Readers with ideas for automotive books, or books on other transport or related hobby subjects are invited to write to the editorial director of Veloce Publishing at the above address.

British Library Cataloguing in Publication Data -
A catalogue record for this book is available from the British Library.

Typesetting (Soutane 10 pt), design and page make-up all by Veloce on Apple Mac.

Printed and bound in England.

Contents

Acknowledgements & Preface

I would like to thank many people and organisations who took the time to help me by providing me with information and illustrations - their help has been much appreciated. Many thanks to Richard for his line illustrations. I would especially like to thank - Allen & Unwin; Annice Collett of the National Motor Museum Library; Brian Dickenson; Fiat Auto (UK) Ltd; Ford Motor Company Limited; H G Mackenzie-Wintle; Metropolitan Police Museum; Mobil Oil Company Limited; Morris Marina/Ital Owners Club; Morris Minor Centre Limited; Morris Minor Owners Club; Morris Register; *Observer*; Mike Redway/ Redrock Records; Renault Owners Club (750/4CV Register); Sears, Roebuck & Co.; Barney Sharratt/Austin A30-A35 Owners Club; Shell UK Limited; Heon Stevenson; Tatra Technical Museum; Ann Tempest/*Daily Mail*; Triumph Mayflower Club; Union Pacific Railroad Company; Van den Bergh Foods Limited; Vauxhall Motors Limited; *Autocar* (Haymarket Magazines); BBC; British Motor Industry Heritage Trust (Rover Group); Henry Ford Museum, Dearborn, USA; Layston Productions Limited; *Maidenhead Advertiser*; National Motor Museum, Beaulieu; National Railway Museum, York.

Many years ago my aunt and uncle owned a Series II Morris Minor - a black, four-door saloon with red seats - and, even now, I have abiding memories of this particular car.

Therefore, long before I was able to drive, I had developed a soft spot for the "Moggie" Minor and, after passing my test, decided that, if I couldn't afford an Alfa Romeo, then I wanted a Morris Minor.

The Minor was generally considered a good choice for several reasons: low insurance costs; ease of driving, repair and maintenance, reliability and cheap, readily available parts. At this point, then, TTA 436H was acquired for a relatively minor sum of money (no pun intended).

The car was in a sorry state and required a great deal of work: if this had been any other late, two-door Minor saloon, it would not have been worth salvaging on economic grounds. However, as an ex-Devon and Cornwall Constabulary Panda car built in 1970, it was considered worth saving because of its rarity. Now, after much time and expense, TTA 436H is finally almost completely restored to original condition.

As a result of my interest in the car I decided to examine the Minor's design and impact since it first appeared in 1948. The end result of this research is intended to be of interest to not only Morris Minor enthusiasts, but also those who are interested in industrial design and the social effects of the motor car.

Karen Pender
Swindon, England

Introduction

The postwar Morris Minor, designed by Alec Issigonis, is one of the best-loved and most charismatic British cars ever invented. Indeed, there are few people who do not instantly recognise the car's distinctive bulbous lines.

There were several reasons why I chose to write about the Morris Minor. Firstly, the Minor was particularly significant because it was the first British car to sell over a million examples. Secondly, it had an extremely long production run which lasted from 1948 until the early 1970s: a period of time which saw many changes in British society as a whole. Finally, as the owner of one of these cars (and member of the Morris Minor Owners Club), I'm aware of the affection that this particular car has inspired in many of its owners. All of these are good reasons for looking at the Morris Minor in some detail.

I've tried to make this work a social history of the Morris Minor, a close look at the interrelationship between postwar British society and one particular car model. An examination that shows how the Minor's design was subject to American and European influences and how it related to other contemporary examples of industrial design. Having looked at society's influence on the Minor's design, I've then researched the Minor's influence on society from the employment it provided, its relationship with the environment, through to the affection it has inspired and which is manifest in songs, poems and the car's continuing enthusiastic following.

I have used many different types of illustration in my book because I feel that pictures are essential in dealing with an example of what Armi refers to as "arguably the most dominant visual form of our century," the motor car.

For readers unfamiliar with automotive terms, a glossary of such terms is included in the appendices.

Karen Pender

Design and design influences

Mr Minor - Alec Issigonis

The Morris Minor has frequently been described by writers as typifying 'Englishness.' A New Zealand journalist in 1977 referred to the car as being "as English as tweed suits and country walks." A broadcaster on the *South Of Watford* television programme described the Minor as being "as English as roast beef and Yorkshire pudding and as reliable as rain at a test match." However, ironically, the designer of the car was not English but Greek.

Alec Issigonis (later Sir Alec), was born in Smyrna (now called Izmir) in 1906, the only son of a Greek father (who had become a naturalised British subject before the First World War) and a German mother. In postwar Smyrna, Issigonis saw motor cars for the first time - these were usually Model T Fords or Overlands - but, according to Barker & Harding, the car that made "a lasting impression on the boy Issigonis was a V-8 Cadillac." The Turkish invasion of Smyrna, in 1922, led to the Issigonis family leaving Greece and settling in England where Alec studied engineering at the Battersea Polytechnic, managing to scrape through an engineering diploma course. A degree had been out of the question because Alec was handicapped by his previously erratic schooling and his lack of mathematical ability.

Alec Issigonis's first job was in a London drawing office, designing semi-automatic transmissions for cars. Then, around 1933, he went to work for Humber and gained valuable experience of suspension design through experimenting with leaf- and coil spring-type independent front suspension systems. In this period, in his spare time, Issigonis designed and built his own racing car called the Lightweight Special. Independent front and rear suspension gave the racer excellent road holding ability. Competition experience developed Issigonis's knowledge of chassis design and suspension and, as biographer Nahum notes, both the Morris Minor and later the Mini were "distinguished by roadholding and 'driveability' which were greatly superior to other contemporary products."

The Secret Life of the Morris Minor

One of the earliest British cars to adopt all steel monocoque construction was the Morris Ten Series M of 1938. Issigonis was involved in the design of the refined, though non-independent, front suspension of this car.

The Nuffield "Gutty." This jeep-like vehicle was a project which Issigonis worked on during the 1940s. It had mechanical similarities with the car range then under development.

Issigonis left Humber in 1936, and went to work for Morris Motors. An early project was his work on the 1938 Morris Ten Series M. Issigonis experimented with rack and pinion steering and independent coil spring and wishbone front suspension but management resisted these innovations. The resistance was partly because of expense and partly because it believed that these new ideas were not adequately refined for production. Thus, the Series M Ten did not have these new features which would later appear on the Y-type MG saloon in 1947. The Series M Ten did, however, appear with a sophisticated design of beam axle front suspension. It was also the first Morris car without a separate chassis frame.

During the second world war, the Morris company - like most other manufacturers - turned to the manufacture of war equipment and machinery. Issigonis, as designer, became involved in a number of war-related projects, such as the amphibious wheelbarrow, which never reached the production stage. He was also involved in the design of a lightweight reconnaissance vehicle (a kind of Jeep) for the Ministry of Defence which was actually produced.

After designing the Minor, Issigonis designed a number of other best-selling British cars, including the Mini - one of the cultural symbols of 1960s Britain - and the BMC 1100/1300. As biographer Nahum remarks, he was "the best-known British car designer and virtually the only one with an international reputation."

The Mosquito

From the early 1940s, Miles Thomas, the new managing director and vice-chairman of the Nuffield Organisation, was starting to think in terms of a range of new car designs for the Morris company once the war was over. He was keen to develop a new, cheap saloon which would seat four people. A vehicle of this type, Thomas believed, offered the Morris company its brightest hope of selling vast numbers of cars to the masses at home and abroad. In his opinion "the Morris Eight was rapidly becoming out of date." It was clear that a new design was needed to replace what had been the best selling car before the war (a total c.394,000 Morris Eights had been sold by the time production - latterly commercial vehicles

- finally ceased in 1953). This volume demand for small cars was a crucial factor leading to the development of the Mosquito and, subsequently, the Minor. Though Lord Nuffield himself disliked the Minor, it "satisfied his desire for a small car which" he believed, offered "great demand possibilities in the future."

Perceived demand for a small, post-war car as seen by directors, management and design staff of Morris Motors, influenced certain factors of its design. In his history of the British motor industry, Adeney noted that, historically, the British have always had a "penchant for small cars" such as the Austin Seven and that "this liking was affected, but not entirely caused by the curiosities of the horsepower tax." Issigonis and directors such as Thomas believed, correctly, that petrol rationing would not be dropped immediately at the end of the war. They felt there would be a vast, ready market for a small, up-to-date four-seater, cheap to buy and cheap to run.

An early Morris Eight, designed to compete with the contemporary small Ford from which it had been largely copied.

Issigonis commented on the importance of economy factors on the design of the car in The Nuffield Exhibits sales brochure of 1949. At a time when other manufacturers were looking towards larger cars, he noted that the Nuffield organisation was more cautious in its outlook - the new model, the Minor, followed its predecessor, the Morris Eight, in providing its owner with "economical motoring" and "the lowest possible upkeep cost."

Issigonis was instructed by Miles Thomas and Vic Oak, the Chief Engineer, to design a new small, economical car as part of a range of larger models. As the designer, he was part of a small team which included two design draughtsmen: Reg Job (who worked on the bodywork) and Jack Daniels (who worked on suspension and chassis details). The team was also helped by several detail-draughtsmen in order to prepare detail drawings for production. This arrangement was generally different to other design offices, both in Britain and in the USA because, usually, in other firms, these departments were much larger. Car designs were generally produced by large committees, not by one individual.

In America, the car designer was a 'stylist,' only concerned with the appearance of the car. As Sparke comments in her study of design and culture, "the engineer worked on the engine while the 'designer' was exclusively concerned with the body." Thus, the American car designers referred to by Armi in his book *The Art Of American Car Design*, such as Harley Earl, were actually stylists. Issigonis, on the other hand, was concerned with the design of the whole vehicle - with car bodywork as well as engine and mechanical parts. He always considered himself to be first and foremost an engineer, and not a stylist on American lines. Issigonis was proud of the fact that he designed every part of the Minor himself - "even the little knob that opens the glove box." Unlike most modern cars, the Morris Minor was the concept of one man - Alec Issigonis. As Jack Daniels said of the Morris Minor "the idea was an Issigonis idea completely."

Between 1943 and 1948 eight prototypes for the new small car - codenamed "Mosquito," appeared. The actual shape of these prototypes differed very little from the eventual production Minor. Features of the Minor that would differ from the Morris Eight Series E it was replacing included smaller (14 inch) wheels, unitary-construction body (no separate chassis), rack and pinion steering and torsion-bar, independent front suspension.

The major differences between early prototypes and the production car of 1948 were windscreen height, grille styling, rear suspension, width of the car and the engine and gearbox. The predominant factors relating to these design changes seem to have been economic ones. As Skilleter remarks, "the whole philosophy of the Mosquito revolved around it being cheaper to make and sell than the Morris Eight." However, political factors outside and within the company, along with the aesthetic considerations of the designer, Alec Issigonis, also played a part in the changes that were made.

The decision to change the windscreen (making it 3/4 inch deeper) was made for practical reasons, to compensate for changes in seating arrangements. The grille was changed by the designer largely for aesthetic reasons. It started as an oval shape with the headlamps behind its vertical slats but evolved into a rectangular-shaped grille with built-in headlamps on the production Series MM. This change provided better road illumination than having the headlamps hidden behind the grille would have done. The bonnet louvres - which were needed on early prototypes to aid the cooling of experimental, horizontal engines with the radiators situated behind - were not needed on the actual production Minor with its conventional in-line unit. A chrome-plated grille was used only on early Minors until 1951 and, from that time onwards, a painted grille was introduced (the plated grille available only as an optional extra). This change was made by company accountants in an attempt to reduce costs. Several different rear suspension systems were experimented with, including independent rear suspension arrangements. Some of these appeared to be fairly promising, but were abandoned mainly because of costs and lack of development time. Thus, the actual production car of 1948 had a commonplace live axle with leaf springs.

The decision to make the production car four inches wider than originally intended, was made purely on aesthetic grounds - because it was thought that the car looked too narrow. It is known that the prototypes handled well, but Jack Daniels believes that the production car was more stable on the road and that the additional width improved the Minor's handling and roadholding qualities. This change also gave the car more interior space for its occupants. However, the last minute decision to make the car wider was only permitted because the directors were informed that the car could be produced at a cost per body not significantly exceeding that of the original narrow version as well as a tool charge for the change. As Wood notes in his book *Wheels of Misfortune* "a ridge in the bonnet, and the front bumper which contained a necessary distance piece, were the only giveaways" on early Minors of the drastic modification which had been made to the original width of the car.

A number of experimental engines and gearboxes were tried out. Less serious experiments were made with a two-stroke engine; however, this smoked and was too thirsty. The RAC horse-power tax was influential on the design of a flat-four, horizontally opposed engine. This was because under the RAC system road tax was based on estimated horsepower (the number of cylinders multiplied by the square of the bore in inches). The design team were therefore directed to build an engine of 800cc for the home market (thus attracting low rates of taxation under the RAC system) which could be bored out to 1100cc for the export market.

In 1946, Issigonis and Miles Thomas, with the aid of some wooden models, helped to lobby the new Labour Chancellor of the Exchequer, Dr. Hugh Dalton, to change this old system of taxation, as it restricted car engine design and penalised the size of an engine - encouraging the building of less rugged, long-stroke engines. When the old Horsepower Tax was abolished in 1947, the new Morris Minor could have an engine size larger than 800cc without affecting its tax status so the directors decided to use the existing vertical four-cylinder (918cc) engine and four-speed gearbox from

The Morris Mosquito. This head-on view of the car which eventually became the Morris Minor accentuates the narrowness of the early prototypes, whilst also showing the different stylistic features including the large plated grille with headlamps behind it. Just visible are the bonnet louvres on the top of the bonnet.

the Morris Eight. There were several reasons for this decision. Mainly, of course, there were cost advantages and savings to be made - but also the engine and gearbox were readily available and had proved to be reliable during the lifetime of the Morris Eight Series E. The experimental engine and gearbox intended for the Minor had not been fully developed: the prototype flat-four engine was not robust; the 800cc engine lacked power and had insufficient torque to cope with the three-speed gearbox (steering column gear change) envisaged. The old engine and gearbox fitted easily into the new Minor's bodyshell and seemed to perform in a satisfactory manner. Using a tried and tested unit meant that long periods of testing would not be necessary.

Political factors within the company also affected the development of prototypes. The chairman, Lord Nuffield, disliked the new, rounded cars - particularly because they "did not have a traditional radiator," and referred to the Mosquito as a "poached egg." It is stated that Lord Nuffield "would not utter the name Issigonis, referring only to 'that foreign chap.'" William Morris met Issigonis on just two occasions, and only had the decency to thank him for his work when a million Minors had been produced. Lord Nuffield wanted to continue with the Morris Eight - and a prototype Eight was built incorporating some Mosquito features, such as rack and pinion steering and independent front suspension. However, this was rejected on grounds of cost and time. Lord Nuffield resisted introducing the Minor until 1948.

The Secret Life of the Morris Minor

The Minor's immediate predecessor, which provided the reliable engine and gearbox for the Series MM, was the Morris Eight Series E shown here. This differed from the early Eight in having a four-speed gearbox and more flowing lines.

It is doubtful that, without the intervention of managing director Miles Thomas, and his successor Reginald Hanks, that the Mosquito, renamed the Minor in 1947, would ever have appeared at all. Indeed, Thomas refers to his long, protracted struggle with Lord Nuffield to get the Minor into production in his autobiography, *Out On A Wing*. The name of the new car was changed from Mosquito because the latter was already used by other companies for their products - including the famous fighter bomber aircraft. Lord Nuffield preferred the new name, which harked back to his Minor of the 1920s.

American influences

Issigonis has acknowledged that he was going through his so-called "American phase" when he designed the Morris Minor - "all voluptuous curves, front mudguards extended into the door panels and 'vee' windscreens." However, the Minor was not just a scaled down American car - the proportions were totally correct. Reg Job, one of the design team, described the car as being a "beautiful shape," but "impossible to alter." Any attempt by the designers to change the shape, even slightly, spoilt it completely. During this era, most British and other European car drivers were accustomed to the perpendicular styling of European cars (Austins, Citroens, Mercedes, Rovers, etc.) There were a few fastback designs, such as Tatra and Hanomag cars, but the rear shapes of these vehicles were totally different from the rear shape of the Minor.

The concept of streamlining in industrial design became popular in 1930s America and came to be known as "streamform." Its leading proponents included Norman Bel Geddes and Raymond Loewy. New, cheaper production methods such as steel stamping and die-casting enabled designers to produce curved radii and bulbous forms for a range of different products from automobiles and locomotives to domestic goods such as refrigerators, ovens, irons and even meat-slicers. Rounded corners and clean curves on automobiles and locomotives were seen as being more aerodynamic and the whole concept of streamlining came to symbolize aspiration and progress, even for domestic items like ovens and refrigerators. As Mclellan has noted, American car designers began to have an increasing influence on the ideas of European car designers from about the middle of the 1930s - helped by improvements in the field of communications. American car designers "began to create a new approach to styling, by turning pressed steel's need for deep curves, swages and mouldings into important styling features rather than the expensive additional decoration they had always been considered before." Early sales brochures emphasized aerodynamic influences on the design of the Morris Minor. "The New Morris Cars" sales brochure of July 1949 referred to the new Minor's "air-flow body lines," its "clean lines" and "flush-fitting door handles." Its curved design was clearly derived from the American concept of streamlining.

A Morris Minor saloon from the late 1920s. Other than the name, this Wolseley-inspired car had nothing in common with the postwar Morris Minor with which this book is concerned.

Most American cars from the late Thirties and early Forties have similar curves to those seen on the Morris Minor. In fact, if you watch films from this era, and own a Morris Minor, you may well get the feeling that something seems vaguely familiar. This is because American cars of this period seem to have the appearance of monster Minors. Certain styling features resemble some of those of the Morris Minor. Although many American cars of this era share similar styling features to those of the British car, the styling of General Motors automobiles (Cadillacs, Chevrolets, Buicks, Oldsmobiles and Pontiacs) seems to have been particularly influential on the Minor's design. The 1941 Packard

The 1930s Tatra T87 model was one of the few exceptions to the prevailing, somewhat upright styling then current in Europe during this era. With an air-cooled V8 rear engine, its obvious influence later became apparent on the Porsche-designed VW Beetle.

Clipper had a considerable impact on European postwar car design, moving as far as possible to the full pontoon style while still retaining vestiges of the separate front and rear wing outline. In Italy, Farina and Touring models, and Sunbeam Talbot's 80 and 90 series in Britain, showed the new styling features of this American car. The 1941 Packard Clipper had flush front and rear wing lines and flared out door sills, like those on the Minor. Flared out door sills were also seen on 1942 automobiles, such as Hudsons and Chevrolets.

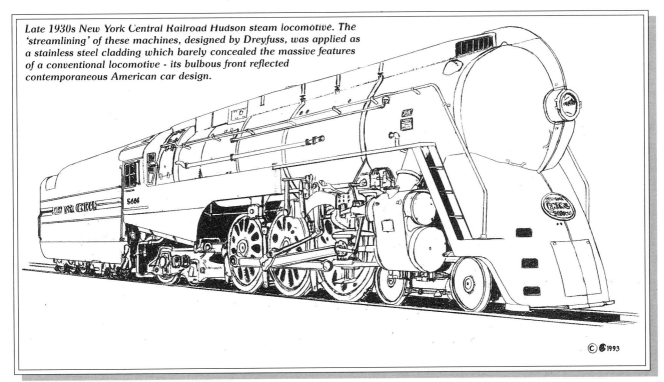

Late 1930s New York Central Railroad Hudson steam locomotive. The 'streamlining' of these machines, designed by Dreyfuss, was applied as a stainless steel cladding which barely concealed the massive features of a conventional locomotive - its bulbous front reflected contemporaneous American car design.

The Secret Life of the Morris Minor

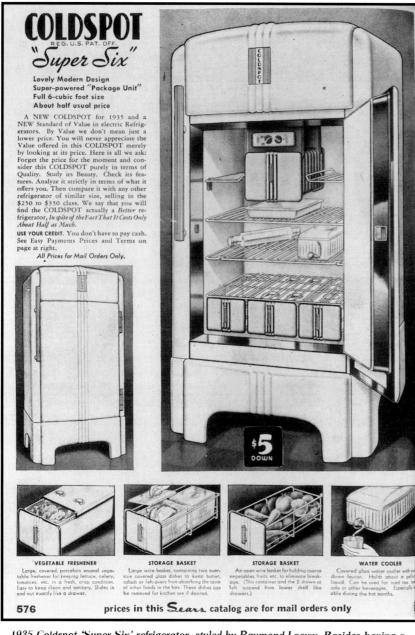

1935 Coldspot 'Super Six' refrigerator, styled by Raymond Loewy. Besides having a name suggestive of a car model, it had styling features similar to those applied to contemporary US cars.

Right: 1940s Coca Cola drink dispenser styled by Raymond Loewy shows the spread of quasi-streamlining into the area of static goods. It has clean curves and faired-in features such as the handle on top, typical of automobile design.

Rounded bonnet curves were seen on 1942 Oldsmobiles and Cadillacs. Rounded roof and boot lines were features of 1940 Oldsmobiles and Studebakers and 1941 Nash models. (The Nash was of unitary construction and had four doors like the Minor). The front grille on the 1941 Willys was very similar in appearance to that found on the Morris Minor Series MM. The 1938 Cadillac had thin door pillars and bright metal window frames, just like those the Minor featured in its design. Issigonis' creation featured a waist moulding with the door handle incorporated in it - similar to the 1940 Studebaker Champion models.

The interior of an early Series MM Minor also shows American influences in its design. The fascia differs markedly from that of its predecessor, the Morris Eight Series E, and from the typically functional fascias of other pre-war European cars. The wider, styled fascia of the Minor, featuring chrome-plating and gold painted steel, closely resembled the styled fascias of late 1930s/early 1940s American cars. An early prototype left-hand-drive Minor of 1947 had featured octagonally-shaped instruments. The actual Series MM Minor when produced in 1948 had a round speedometer and a round badge (which covered the space for an optional clock). There was a heav-

the most economical <u>REAL CAR</u> in the World!

AIR-FLOW BODY LINES: Sheer, wind-cheating lines mean good looks *and economy*. Flush-fitting door handles, sloping "V" windscreen, clean lines—all these items lessen air drag, make the car's passage smoother, thereby using less power.

Above: From The New Morris Cars *sales brochure of 1949, the silhouette of the Minor demonstrates airflow over the body in order to publicize the aerodynamic lines of the car - a feature more usually associated with advertising cars of the 1980s onwards.*

Above & left: American styling influences. The picture above shows an early 1940s Oldsmobile saloon, with the generally bulbous lines of American cars of the immediate pre-war period. This example is particularly relevant being a saloon with a bustle tail, domed bonnet top, faired in wings and swept out door bottoms. Left: all these features are clearly evident on the Series MM saloon.

The Secret Life of the Morris Minor

1941 Willys "Americar." The horizontal grille seen on this particular car has distinct similarities with the proportions of that fitted to the Series MM Morris Minor.

ily sculpted chrome panel in the centre of the dash, with the control knobs placed beneath it. This had been influenced by styled, American fascia designs.

The Morris Minor Traveller, or estate car version, which was produced from October 1953, is usually thought of as being typically British with its half-timbered effect, but the inspiration for this model came largely from America. The "Woodie" station wagon was extremely popular in the US in the Thirties. There were many

American styling influences. Right: the Buick fascia panel from the late 1930s, its prominent central grille feature is an example of the inspiration for the styling of the early Morris Minor fascia, below.

American styling influences. During the pre-war era, the most popular station wagons were manufactured by Ford. The 1939 example of the Ford V8 "Woodie," (above) shows the typically bulbous styling features of American cars of this era, combined with timber construction of much of the bodywork. Whilst retaining the exposed timber framing so characteristic of the Woodie, Issigonis sought to reduce manufacturing costs by incorporating painted metal rather than varnished timber for the panels in the rear section of the Morris Traveller body, pictured below . (Ford photograph from the collections of Henry Ford Museum and Greenfield Village).

The Secret Life of the Morris Minor

The car above is from the early years of production with the headlamps in the position that Issigonis intended. The car below has the headlamps in the later raised position, originally introduced in order to comply with American vehicle lighting regulations.

variants, but Ford and their Mercury station wagons, were perhaps the best known. However, the British version of the woodie, the Morris Traveller, featured both wooden frames and aluminium panels in its construction process. The American woodie, on the other hand, had more timber (or later, plastic) in its design and the whole body of the vehicle from the start of the front door was built out of wood (apart from metal rear wings and fabric roof).

It is worth noting at this point the reaction of an American car designer towards the new Morris Minor (which resembled a baby American car in its styling). Jack Daniels remembers the 1948 Motor Show, when the Minor appeared for the first time in front of the general public. He recalls that the Chief Engineer of General Motors, America, looked closely at the new Minor and came up to congratulate Alec Issigonis "for the most effective way he had produced the car with the space it had in the size it had." This was evidently a great compliment to Issigonis - his new design had earned the praise of a top American engineer.

A major influence on early Morris Minor Series MM models was Californian headlamp legislation, which meant that North American export Minors from late 1949 had to have the headlamps fitted on the top of the front wings of the car. There were rumours that this legislation might spread to Europe, so the manufacturers decided to rationalize, and all post-1950-51 Minors showed the new arrangement. Issigonis did not like this enforced change. In fact, the new headlamp arrangement reduced the top speed of early Series MM Minors by about 1.5mph!

American influences also affected other examples of industrial design in postwar Britain. For example, the LMS diesel-electric locomotives nos 10000 and 10001, were heavily influenced by General Motors locomotive designs - and showed the American-type cab and nose. Also, American culture was influential on other aspects of life in postwar British society and continued to influence mass culture throughout the 1950s. In her study of design and culture, Sparke refers to the import of American culture as "cocacolanization." American films, popular music, clothing and pulp fiction - together with American-type advertising and consumerism - flooded into Britain during this period. Milk bars with jukeboxes playing rock and roll music emerged throughout Britain during this era. The teddy boy culture was clearly conditioned by young people becoming increasingly exposed to new ideas imported from America. There is no evidence, however, that Morris Minor owners themselves were consciously adopting American influences, ideas and attitudes when they purchased the new car, even if it was styled along American lines. Advertising of the Morris Minor in the 1940s and 1950s was aimed at the typical British middle-class family.

European influences

Although the shape of the Morris Minor was derived from American models of the late Thirties and early Forties aspects of its mechanical design were derived from earlier European models. Certain French and Italian models appear to have been particularly influential in this respect.

The American cars mentioned earlier were, mechanically, very different vehicles from the Morris Minor. One of the few things most shared with the Morris Minor Series MM models of 1948 were sidevalve engines, and live rear axles. American cars of this era were physically much larger cars than the diminutive Minor. They had huge 6, 8 or even twelve-cylinder engines (the

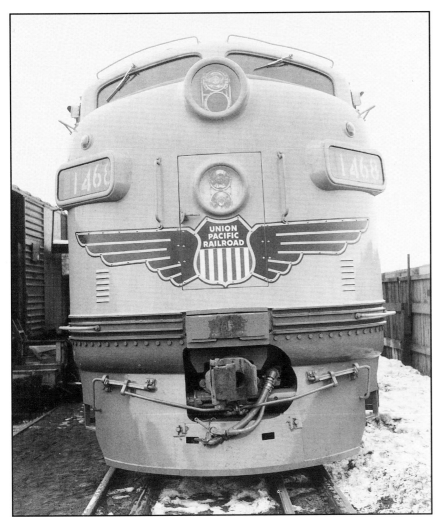

American styling influences. Left: the ubiquitous face of a first generation diesel locomotive supplied by General Motors to the US railroad industry, showing the high set driver's windscreens behind a bulbous nose. Below: Number 10,000 of the London, Midland, and Scottish Railway was delivered new from the Derby locomotive works in 1947 and, as such, was the first main line British diesel locomotive. Visual similarities are apparent in the styling of the cab ends.

The Secret Life of the Morris Minor

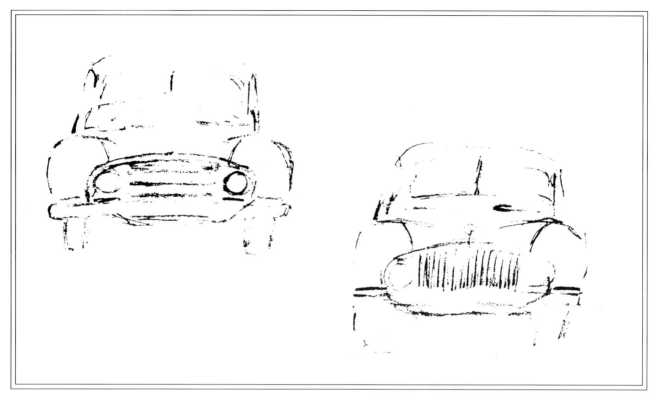

The Minor takes shape. A couple of Alec Issigonis' original design sketches.

Minor's engine had only four cylinders) and most were of over 4-litres capacity (compared with 918cc for a Series MM Minor). Average fuel consumption figures for most American cars were between 15 and 20 miles per gallon, compared with 36-40mpg for an early Series MM. Handling was completely different, American cars of this era were designed chiefly for comfort - to carry passengers along rough roads and over far greater distances than their European counterparts. They were far more softly sprung than the British car, and usually had coil-spring independent suspension at the front, and semi-elliptic springs and live axle at the back. Handling qualities tended to be indifferent. Sedgwick refers to the "soggy independent suspensions" of many American cars of this period. The separate chassis and three-speed, column-mounted gearchange of the typical American car compared poorly with the unitary body and four-speed floor change of the Minor. Steering on these American cars was usually of the conventional steering box arrangement, which tended to be vague when compared with the rack and pinion arrangement used on the Minor. A journalist in the US *Motor Trend* magazine of April 1961 was full of praise for the Morris 1000 model, remarking that the rack-and-pinion steering was "light and accurate, one of the reasons the car handles as beautifully as it does at all speeds." He also noted the excellent gearchange: it moved "up through the four gears with all the alacrity of a sports car."

The foregoing shows that whilst the styling characteristics of American cars were appropriate for the new Minor, the same could not be said of mechanical features.

Two of the most influential European cars in the Thirties were the Fiat 500

Sectional illustration of a 1930s Fiat 500 "Topolino," clearly showing the forward-mounted position of the engine. This is reproduced from 1930s Fiat sales literature.

The Fiat 500 "Topolino" was introduced in 1937. It possessed good handling qualities owing to its independent front suspension and lightweight construction.

A late 1930s example of the Citroen Traction Avant. The car has generally conservative styling typical of the 1930s when it was designed. The body conceals much technical innovation.

The Secret Life of the Morris Minor

Topolino and the Citroen *Traction Avant*. Issigonis was a great admirer of French-designed cars, particularly Citroens and another member of the Minor design team, Jack Daniels, has commented that Issigonis had Citroen cars available to him at the Cowley factory.

The position of the Minor's power unit, with the forward-mounted engine (ahead of the front wheels) in a 'nose-heavy' arrangement was possibly derived from the popular Fiat 500 Topolino. This car was produced in vast numbers between 1936 and 1948, and was the smallest mass-produced vehicle in the world during this period. Its diminutive size caused the general public to give it the nickname of "*Topolino*" or "little mouse." Like the Morris Minor, the Fiat 500 was noted for its superb handling qualities and lack of body roll.

Some distinctive features of the 1948 Morris Minor were probably derived from Sedgwick's choice of the "car of the decade" of the 1930s, the Citroen Traction Avant. The Citroen was one of the first cars to be produced without a separate chassis. Apart from front wheel drive, it boasted rack and pinion steering, which was precise and responsive, and independent torsion-bar front suspension: the latter giving these cars the good handling and extraordinary roadholding for which the Tractions were to become famous. These steering and suspension features were seen on the Minor of 1948 and helped to give it good handling too.

European influences affected other aspects of life in postwar Britain. France had dominated pre-war design, but after 1945 was no longer the dominant influence. The major exception to this was in the field of fashion. Dior's 'New Look' dominated the 1950s. A new feminine look for women, with nipped-in waists and full, long skirts contrasted with the padded shoulders and shorter skirts of the austerity era. Scandinavian glass, jewellery and furniture were popular from the Fifties. Marwick notes that Scandinavian influences were "heavily in evidence" in British industrial designs throughout the 1950s. From the late Fifties, though, Italian culture and the "'cool' Continental-style dominated British popular taste." Teenagers wore stiletto heels and winkle-picker shoes, rode on Vespa and Lambretta motor-scooters, and crowded into espresso coffee bars.

Jaguar XK120 roadster. This particular car was the exotic star of the 1948 British Motor Show, as one would expect. However, judging from the crowds around it at the show, the Morris Minor would appear to have been the more attainable.

Debut

The Morris Minor Series MM was first introduced to the general public at the British Motor Show of 1948. It was part of a range of new Nuffield cars which included the Morris Oxford (Series MO), the Morris Six (Series MS) and the Wolseley Six-Eighty and Four-Fifty models. The 1948 Motor Show was the first one to be held for ten years, due to the second world war. An insatiable demand for cars, and great interest in them built up during the car-rationed years of the war. It is no wonder, then, that this particular Motor Show was visited by "over half a million people - more than double any pre-war attendance," according to Plowden.

The new Jaguar XK120 may have stolen the 1948 Motor Show as the most attractive and impressive-looking new sports car, but the new Morris Minor attracted more attention than any other new saloon car. The new small car was an instant success - its stand was packed with people who were keen to look at the new Nuffield model.

The Morris Minor was described as "the show sensation" by journalists writing in the *Motor* magazine. There were a number of reasons why the new car received praise and compliments from both journalists and members of the public alike. First of all, the distinctive styling of the Minor was perceived as being attractive and modern-looking - *Autocar* called it a "triumph in good looks." The Minor was unique - it looked like no other car. Then there were the car's mechanical features, which gave it such good handling and steering qualities and set new standards in the small saloon car class.

In a straight line, the Minor's acceleration was no better than most of its contemporaries (see Appendix 2), but a *Motor* journalist, writing in June 1951, remarked that the Minor had "quite exceptional road holding" and that its "cornering powers were equalled by only a few continental sports cars." Before the Minor's appearance, the handling of most small cars had not been very good, but the Minor's popularity quickly proved that the general public wanted good handling qualities in their cars. Other advantages were the car's spacious interior, good fuel economy (in an era of petrol rationing) and competitive price (see Appendix 2). Most other new cars in 1948, like the Jowett Javelin, and Austin A40 and A70 models, were larger and much more expensive to buy: the Jowett, for example, cost approximately twice as much as a Minor. The Ford Anglia and Prefect models were cheaper, but still had pre-war technology and looks.

The tremendous enthusiasm of the motoring press for the new Morris Minor helped to make it such a success. Good press reports about the new small car reached the public before the opening of the Motor Show in 1948 so that at the Show the Minor was completely besieged - one visitor remarked, people could be found "four at a time trying the seating of Cowley's Minor." A cartoon sketch in the *Autocar* magazine of November 1948 showed a crowd of people gathering around the new Morris Minor Series MM saloon.

Demand for the new model was underestimated by the Nuffield organisation. Two new assembly lines had to be put down during the first year of production in order to meet the ever-increasing demand for the new Minor.

Minor versus the rest

The best way of approaching this subject is by comparing the Morris Minor Series MM with contemporary small cars of the early Fifties. These rivals include the Ford Anglia Eight, the Triumph Mayflower, the Austin A30 and the Renault 750 (or 4CV).

The appearance of the Minor, with its clean lines and uncluttered shape, was praised by motoring press and general public alike from the car's introduction in 1948. Design historian Penny Sparke has referred to it as "one of the most successful designs" of postwar Britain. This praise contrasts with contemporary reports describing the Ford Anglia as old-fashioned looking, and the mixed reception by the motoring press for the Triumph Mayflower - which looked like a pocket-sized Rolls-Royce. A *MotorSport* road test on the Austin A30 in 1953 commented that they were not "particularly enamoured" by the car's appearance. Interestingly, the design of the Renault 750 was liked by the

A contemporary cartoon in Autocar *showed the new Morris Minor at the Earls Court Motor Show in October 1948, attracting crowds like ants to a honeypot.*

The Secret Life of the Morris Minor

The early 1950s Triumph Mayflower had, for a small car, unusual "razor-edge" styling. This shortlived design was largely cobbled together from existing Standard-Triumph mechanical parts.

Austin A30. Having failed in his first attempt at taking over Morris Motors, Leonard Lord, Chairman of Austin, introduced the postwar baby Austin in order to compete directly with the Morris Minor. This car embodies the personal animosity between Lord and Nuffield.

British motoring press because of its clean lines, not dissimilar to those of the Minor.

The Minor's rack-and-pinion steering which gave drivers good sensitivity to road conditions, was the same assembly later used in the Austin-Healey Sprite (and MG Midget) sports car produced from 1958 onwards. It is hardly surprising then, that an *Autocar* road test of 1948 awarded "full marks" to the Minor, for "suspension, steering, stability and general roadworthiness." The suspension gave a good ride when compared to the choppy ride experienced by road testers of the Ford Anglia in 1949 with its transverse leaf springs and beam axle. The Anglia was also limited by a three-speed gearchange and technology dating back to the 1928 Model A Ford. Road tests of the Austin A30, in the early Fifties, complained about the lack of feel in the car's steering, whilst *MotorSport* in 1953 remarked that the A30 did not have "such good controllability as its near-relation, the Morris Minor." The Renault 750, like the Minor, had precise rack-and-pinion steering and was described as being pleasant to drive. However, having a rear engine in a light car meant that, when it was driven hard, the back wheels tended to "break away on a curve." The Triumph Mayflower's suspension was extremely comfortable - but the three-speed, steering column-mounted gearchange would not have helped to give the car sporting appeal.

The amount of interior space in a small car is an important design feature (emphasised by Issigonis in his later design, the Mini). It has been well documented that Issigonis was obsessed with the idea of compactness in all his many car designs and of obtaining the most from the least. Jack Daniels has referred to this philosophy as getting "the smallest car with the biggest payload" (or largest amount of interior space). The decision to use smaller diameter road wheels, (14 inch instead of the 17 inch wheels used on the Morris Eight Series E) enabled the designer to increase the amount of space inside the Minor when compared with its predecessor.

Early road tests praised the amount of internal space inside the new Minor. It would seat four adults easily and take three people in the back at a push. The luggage compartment of seven cubic feet capacity was described as being of useful size by road testers. The car's roominess was constantly emphasized

Small Fords dating from the immediate postwar era to the late 1950s were of archaic design. In spite of this, they sold well owing to their low purchase prices and good servicing facilities.

Right: The Renault 750 (or 4CV) was a competitor to the Morris Minor for much of its production life. Surprisingly, this small French car was assembled in London for the UK market, thereby avoiding punitive import duties: despite this it remained more expensive than the Minor.

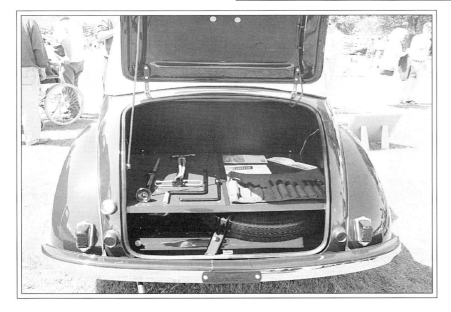

A Morris Minor Series MM convertible showing the amount of luggage space available. The tools visible are those supplied with early cars and normally these items would be stowed in a tool roll adjacent to the spare wheel.

Late sales brochure, illustrating the continuing emphasis on the Minor's luggage space. Although a boot capacity of 7 cubic feet was barely adequate by the standards of the 1960s, when the car was introduced in 1948 it was a considerable advance on the facilities offered by pre-war cars.

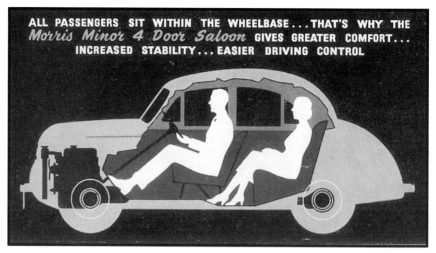

1952 sales brochure diagram emphasizing the spaciousness of the car's accomodation for occupants and clearly illustrating the large amount of headroom available for hat wearers.

in sales brochures throughout the Minor's production life and its good headroom enabled many police forces to use Morris Minors as Panda (patrol) cars during the 1960s and early 1970s: the car's high roofline meant that officers could wear their helmets whilst driving. The Ford Anglia was much narrower than the Morris Minor, being derived from the pre-war era. The Triumph Mayflower, whilst being spacious, was a much longer and wider car than the Minor. The Renault 750 and Austin A30 were both smaller cars than the Minor. They could seat four adults, but anyone over six foot tall in the back seats would be cramped and the Minor's luggage capacity far exceeded that of these two cars.

Other strongly competitive aspects of the Minor's design included good fuel economy - which was important in the postwar era of petrol rationing - and a realistic purchase price. Later versions of the Minor continued both these trends. Although the Morris Minor was not the cheapest car in 1953, the Triumph Mayflower and Renault 750 were considerably more expensive to purchase.

One of the best features of the new Morris Minor was that it was easy to maintain and had good engine accessibility: ideal for the practical owner who liked to service and repair the car at home. The new Morris Minor appealed both to the diy mechanic and to suburban, middle-class people who wanted a "nice little car." The rear-engined Renault 750 was also praised by motoring journalists because of its good engine accessibility and ease of maintenance. The Austin A30's engine was less accessible than the Minor's, owing to the small size of its engine compartment.

The reliability of the Morris Minor, generally, was excellent. In a *MotorSport* magazine survey of Morris Minor owners in 1962, nearly 80 per cent of all owners interviewed stated they would buy the same car again. Interestingly, of those who were surveyed, the majority of the 20 per cent who said they would not buy a Minor again, named a German VW as their next choice of car purchase.

There were, of course, some bad aspects of the Morris Minor's design.

However, as we will see, these were not major structural faults and, fortunately, modifications were made early on in the car's life. This compares favourably with a number of other British contemporaries - some of which had serious design faults.

Early teething problems with the Minor were generally sorted out by the manufacturer soon after its introduction in 1948. The most serious fault was the appearance of cracks in the toeboard of some cars, next to the top of the gearbox cover. Later models had toeboard reinforcing plates fitted, and this cured the problem. An early problem of knocking front suspension was cured by fitting rubber-bushed top links. The usual problems experienced by most new car models, such as water leaks from windows and doors for example, were cured by modifications made at the Cowley factory.

An annoyance to generations of Minor owners has been the fact that the brake master cylinder was badly sited, being buried within the underfloor body structure on the driver's side of the car. This made it difficult to check the level of the brake fluid (recommended to be carried out every 1000 miles in the owner's workshop manual) and to keep it topped-up. The master cylinder's location also meant that water was able to get in to the brake fluid during bad weather.

Another problem was one of rust, although the Morris Minor was far better than most of its contemporaries in this respect - how many Minor contemporaries do you see driving around now? However, the Minor did suffer (and many still do) from specific problems relating to corrosion. As Skilleter notes, one "particularly bad design fault lay at the rear of the front wings, where a panel joined the outer wing to form a perfect mud trap." This tended to cause a line of corrosion in the wing next to the door and meant

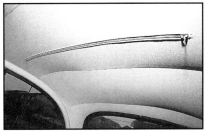

Above: A constable and a sergeant pose with an example of a Metropolitan Police Panda car. Many late 2-door Minors were supplied to police forces throughout the UK for use as patrol cars under the Panda car scheme. Right: In recent years often the only readily identifiable feature of former Panda cars is the zip across the headlining, originally provided to gain access to the wiring of the roof sign and radio aerial.

The Morris Minor had an engine bay designed to accept the inherently wide, horizontally-opposed engine intended for the Mosquito. This has resulted in generous space around the in-line engines which were actually fitted to the Minor - a fact much appreciated by mechanics!

The Secret Life of the Morris Minor

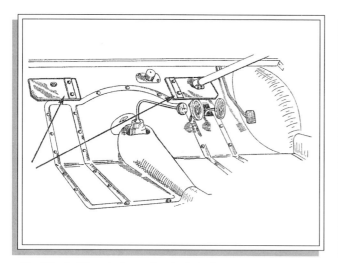

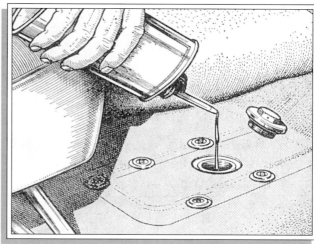

The Morris Minor had very few technical problems on its introduction, but one problem that manifested itself early on was the splitting of the floor around the mounting bolts for the rack and pinion steering unit. This was overcome by adding reinforcement plates as a modification under warranty and incorporating these items in the construction of later cars.

Above, right: Poor siting of brake master cylinder which is "accessible for replenishment through the aperture revealed when the carpet in front of the driver's seat is lifted." Oh, really! Most people would expect to find this item under the bonnet. Below: This photograph shows the final stage of removing the brake master cylinder. It does not show, however, that the adjacent components of the front suspension and clutch pedal have also to be dismantled if one is working strictly to the book. This is probably one of the most unpleasant tasks in maintaining a Minor.

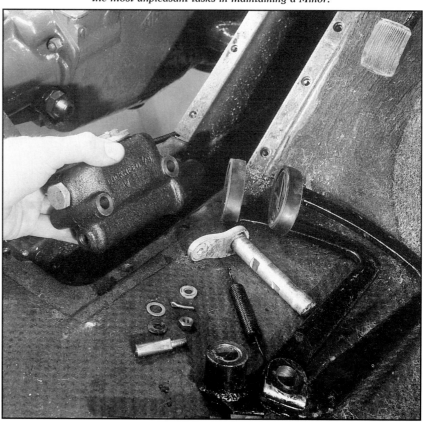

Rust at the rear edge of a Minor's front wing. This is a notorious but superficial fault - there are possibly more serious problems of corrosion festering under the car!

A brave attempt by a small company to build a technologically-advanced modern car in the early postwar years - the Jowett Javelin included many of the features which Issigonis would have liked to incorporate in the Minor (the Jowett's designer, Palmer, being a sometime colleague of Issigonis).

the owner would have to renew the wing (though, at least, this item was bolted-on).

Three other faults were created by design changes made to later models. From 1954, the speedometer was moved to a centrally-mounted position on the dashboard; previously it had been in front of the driver. This change was made as the result of a cost-cutting exercise to facilitate the production of both left-hand and right-hand drive models. The instrument's new position was ergonomically bad and *Autocar* magazine of May 1964 commented that this was "inferior to the facia layout of the original Series MM Minor" and that the driver's left arm on the wheel often obscured the instrument. The seats on later cars were hard (from 1956 onwards) when compared with earlier models, and lacked lateral support. In 1964 *Autocar* remarked that the seating was "pretty firm" and that drivers sat on, not sank into, the seats. The rear suspension on later models exhibited axle tramp under hard driving conditions. This problem was not apparent on the Series MM, but manifested itself when, from 1956 models onwards, the engine size increased to 948cc (then to 1098cc). The *Autocar* magazine of May 1964 commented on "axle hop" causing the "back wheels to run wide" and requiring fast correction from a driver on wet roads.

The problem of worn trunnions, and wheel collapse on elderly Minors, can generally be traced back to poor maintenance by owners. The steering joints (or lower trunnions) must be greased every 1000 miles, according to maintenance literature, to minimise wear.

Generally the faults on the Minor were not too serious, especially when compared with certain other British cars of the same era. Two postwar contemporaries - the Jowett Javelin and the Standard Vanguard - both had major design faults. The Jowett Javelin, for example, suffered from a number of problems, including crankshaft failure, blown gaskets and run bearings. The gearbox tended to jump out of third gear. The low-mounted horizontally-op-

In answer to the postwar demand to "export or die," the Standard Motor Company initially adopted a one model policy with the Vanguard - an early attempt to manufacture a "world car." Unfortunately, it was unable to fully live up to this expectation.

An example of a Morris 1000 convertible showing how all the side windows remain in place even when the hood is lowered.

posed engine was difficult to service and had "excellent self-drowning properties in wet weather," according to Sedgwick. It was not until the Bradford company introduced a series III engine in 1953 that these problems were cured - and, by that time, Jowett were in severe financial difficulty. The Standard Vanguard was another example of a car rushed onto the market without proper testing. Standard company engineers had not taken into account the poor conditions of roads abroad. Early cars were "unable to cope with Continental pave roads" and suffered from huge fractures in the chassis frame, giving "British cars a reputation for unreliability for which they would suffer for decades." Continental manufacturers, such as Volkswagen, were not able to resume large scale manufacturing directly after 1945 and could therefore take longer and put more care into the development of their immediate postwar vehicles.

Design changes

A number of modifications were made to the original Morris Minor design during the car's production life between 1948 and 1971. A range of four different versions was gradually introduced. These were the saloon (2- and 4-door versions), the open tourer (or convertible), the Traveller (or estate car) and the light commercial vehicle (pick-up and van versions). However, apart from occasionally updating the car with improved mechanical parts and engine changes to increase performance, the design of the car did not alter dras-

The Secret Life of the Morris Minor

tically during more than twenty years of production.

Following the Nuffield-Austin merger into the vast British Motor Corporation in 1952, rationalization led to the 803cc ohv Austin engine and transmission being fitted to the Morris Minor. This offered slightly better acceleration

Light commercial vehicles. Above, right: Rear view of the load area of the pick-up showing the generous amount of space for cargo. Below: Interior view of van shows similar construction including the timber floor - then a traditional feature of commercial vehicle bodies.

than the previously fitted sidevalve unit. (There had been several proprietary modifications available for the old 918cc engine, such as the Alta conversion, which improved acceleration and increased top speed to over 70mph). Two further engine changes took place - the use of 948cc (37bhp) and 1098cc (48bhp) ohv units, gave the car increased performance.

Apart from the repositioning of the headlamps (to comply with American legislation), a new single-piece windscreen in place of the split-screen variety, larger rear window, different grille design and larger tail lamps and indicator lights (to replace the early semaphore variety) - the final version of the Minor 1000 looked practically unchanged when compared with an early Series MM. Although production methods in 1948 had made the use of a one-piece windscreen feasible then, British car makers were reluctant to fit them because they were concerned about the glare from a curved windscreen. Also it would probably have cost more to produce curved glass at that time. The changeover to a one-piece windscreen was of great benefit to all Morris Minor owners because the split-screen type window was prone to water leaks and the windscreen wiper failed to wipe all parts of the

Rear view of Series II saloon, showing badge and lights.

windscreen (on early Minors, a second windscreen wiper was only available as an optional extra).

Glovebox lids came and went, as did a variety of steering wheels, in order to suit the whims of BMC cost accountants. BMC rationalization and attempts to reduce costs across their entire range of cars led to many examples of cost-cutting measures on later Minors such as the replacement of leather seats by PVC ones and the cheaper two-spoke steering wheel.

A number of other design changes were brought about by changing legislation. For example, the 1953 Road Transport Lighting Act dictated the minimum size of reflectors and rear lamps and led to the fitting of larger rear lamps on the car. Most export models (North America and Europe) were fitted with flashing indicator lights from the early 1950s in response to regulations. Other features, such as the fitting of seat belt anchorages, were introduced by the manufacturer of the Morris Minor in anticipation of subsequent legislation.

Selling the
Morris Minor

Sales figures for the Morris Minor reflected changing living standards in postwar Britain. The two periods we will examine here are the postwar austerity period and the growth of affluent society. The postwar austerity period lasted approximately from 1945 to the early to mid-1950s, when all rationing was finally abolished. The growth of affluent society took place between about 1957 and the early 1970s.

Export or die

The postwar austerity period is usually associated with rationing (in Britain clothes were rationed until 1949, main food stuffs until 1954 and meat until 1956). As a result of the second world war and the ending of the lend-lease agreement, Britain owed huge economic debts to the USA. British manufacturers were ordered to "export or die" by the Chancellor, Sir Stafford Cripps, to bring in badly needed foreign currency, especially dollars, to pay for imported goods. If car makers did not guarantee to export most of their cars, the British government would not make over to them the quantities of steel that they needed to manufacture their vehicles. Thus, Britain was deliberately starved of cars, with over 75 per cent of her total car output going abroad.

By 1950 Britain had become the world's largest exporter of cars - surpassing even the United States - following the destruction of most Continental European industry during the war. Thus, over 75 per cent of early Morris Minor production was exported, mainly to non-European countries.

The top ten markets for Morris Minor sales up to 1960 were -

Australia .... 101,246 cars
USA .... 52,431 cars
Eire .... 35,492 cars
South Africa .... 34,639 cars
New Zealand .... 34,216 cars

Selling the Morris Minor

Canada .... 29,538 cars
Sweden .... 25,375 cars
Holland .... 20,356 cars
Malaya .... 16,405 cars
Denmark .... 14,213 cars

(Source: Newell, 1982).

By 1960, 479,525 Morris Minors had been sent abroad - amounting to about 48 per cent of the total number manufactured. Even as late as 1969 about 40 per cent of all Minors produced had gone to overseas markets. Home buyers faced long waits, over a year in some cases. The four-door Minor was only available for export markets for a while.

1946 had seen the "Britain Can Make It" exhibition of new industrial designs. This event was a great success with the British public, over a million and a half of them visiting the exhibition. Many new designs from fashion to garden equipment were on display. The overall theme of this event was "swords

Picture from an early Nuffield export brochure, showing a Morris Minor saloon being loaded for its trip across the Atlantic - a fact that can be determined from: a) chrome-plated window frames on the doors and flat bumper blades, denoting that it is an early car and b) the raised position of the headlamps, demanded by US legislation.

The Secret Life of the Morris Minor

into ploughshares," showing how war equipment manufacturers could turn to the production of more peacetime items, as an example, one stand showed the aluminium frame of an aircraft being converted into saucepans. Design was stressed as "creating a hopeful vision of the future" and the exhibition itself was colourful, bright and cheerful. However, most of the items exhibited were either for export only or in the prototype stage and not generally available - this led to the exhibition being dubbed "Britain Can't Have It" by some critics.

Sales grow with postwar prosperity

Sales figures (see appendix 3) for the Morris Minor reflect the growth of Galbraith's affluent society. From the mid-1950s onwards many Minors were sold. This pattern mirrored the growth of average weekly earnings during the period. This era saw the huge growth in ownership of consumer durables such as television sets, washing machines and refrigerators. By the early 1960s, 75 per cent of British households had television sets and 33 per cent had refrigerators (rising to 69 per cent and 91 per cent respectively by 1971) . Marwick remarked that, possibly, "the very visible growth in the acquisition of durable consumer goods was necessary to help workers forget the conditions of the work place."

Rising incomes illustrate the growing affluence of many British workers during the 1950s and 1960s. During the era of Morris Minor production (between 1948 and 1971) the average weekly earnings of men over 21 years of age were as follows -

1951 .... £8.30
1961 .... £15.35
1966 .... £20.30
1968 .... £23.00
1969 .... £24.80
1970 .... £28.05
1971 .... £30.93

(Source: Marwick, 1990).

There was some inflation during this period - retail prices rose by 15 per cent between 1955 and 1960 and were 63 per cent higher in 1969 than they had been in 1955. However, weekly wage rates went up 25 per cent between 1955 and 1960 - and had gone up by 88 per cent in 1969 (figures including overtime payments show even greater gains in weekly earnings for most workers). As Marwick has commented, while the cost of "food and other necessities were steadily rising, the prices of small cars, in relation to earning power, were falling, and the many products of new technology, such as television sets and washing machines, were, despite inflation, actually costing less."

The decline of public transport

Sales figures for the Morris Minor (see appendix 3) reflect other trends in postwar British society - the huge growth in private car ownership and the decline of public transport. This growth of private transport was helped greatly by the falling prices of cars in relation to incomes and the enormous growth in hire purchase. The number of motor vehicles licensed between 1948 and 1968 in

Britain was -

	Private cars & vans	Motorcycles, scooters & mopeds	Public transport vehicles
1948	1,960,510	559,313	127,625
1958	4,548,530	1,519,935	95,680
1968	10,816,100	1,324,400	99,300
	(Source: Halsey, 1972).		

The Morris Minor was the first British car to sell over a million. The millionth car was actually produced in December 1960 and marked a "significant achievement in British motoring" according to Newell. In 1959 the opening stretch of Britain's first motorway, the M1, was opened between London and Birmingham - and by 1971 more than 750 miles of motorway had been completed. During this period an increasing number of heavy goods vehicles appeared (at the expense of the railway freight services) as roads were specially built to accommodate them. The number of motorcycles on British roads declined after 1965, when more people found that they could afford to buy cars

Genius at work. Alec Issigonis, seen here with documents relating to the Minor's design, was a steam enthusiast and made Gauge 1 railway models in his spare time. Ironically, his popular cars contributed to the demise of the railways in Britain.

The Secret Life of the Morris Minor

instead.

Public transport declined drastically throughout the period that Morris Minors were produced (between 1948 and the early 1970s). In 1961 Dr. Beeching was brought on to the new British Railways Board to find out exactly "where the railways were making their enormous losses." As a result of his inquiry, many rural passenger services were found to be uneconomic - and numerous stations and branch lines were subsequently closed down. The railway network was reduced from 18,369 to 15,991 miles by 1964 - with only 11,670 miles remaining open to passenger trains. However, "the profits anticipated by Dr. Beeching did not materialize," according to Bagwell (apart from just two years - 1969 and 1970). In Britain capital investment in the railways has been infinitely smaller than investment in roads. In 1971 British Rail spent £26 million on the maintenance of track - compared with £687 million spent by the government on roads in the same year.

Public bus services have also declined since the early 1950s, faced with intense competition from the private motor car. The 1960s "was a decade of bus closures" according to Bagwell. The number of bus and coach passenger

Year	Rail	Road (public service vehicles)	Public sector (road & rail)	Road (private transport)
1952	21.48	44.65	66.13	33.78
1953	20.58	43.30	63.88	35.95
1954	19.90	41.12	61.02	38.82
1955	18.58	38.88	57.46	42.39
1956	18.43	36.57	55.02	44.77
1957	19.62	34.77	54.39	45.38
1958	17.95	30.54	48.49	51.30
1959	16.77	28.99	45.76	53.98
1960	15.64	27.68	43.32	56.37
1961	14.38	25.72	41.01	59.55
1962	13.18	24.51	37.69	61.91
1963	12.43	23.03	35.46	64.07
1964	11.72	20.53	32.25	67.29
1965	10.54	18.96	29.40	70.00
1966	9.95	17.36	27.31	72.18
1967	9.33	16.28	25.61	73.87
1968	8.81	15.38	24.19	75.30
1969	8.91	14.72	23.63	75.88

Note: this table omits figures for air travel. (Source: Aldcroft, 1974).

Now-you move up TWICE AS FAST!

0-60 mph in 28 secs.

in the mighty **MORRIS** MINOR 1000

Over half-a-million owners know the "Quality First" Morris Minor has always been a pretty brisk mover.

Now, with a new, more powerful 950 c.c. O.H.V. engine, *acceleration has actually been stepped up 100%! Under test the 'Minor 1000' recently recorded 0-60 m.p.h. through the gears in 28.2 seconds, without fuss or effort.*

And this whip-quick acceleration for safer, more responsive driving goes with an economy of fuel and upkeep that is a byword in motoring! In fact, throughout its speed range the Minor 1000 returns a phenomenal mileage per valuable gallon. And you get this economy whilst still enjoying all the pleasures of big-car motoring!

To-day more than ever **THE WORLD'S BIGGEST SMALL CAR BUY**

12 MONTHS' WARRANTY

REMEMBER—your Morris Minor 1000 is backed by B.M.C., biggest producers of cars in Britain, affording the most comprehensive service facilities in Europe.

Quality and dependability are guaranteed by the B.M.C. Used-Car Warranty and you are certain of a good deal when you sell.

MORRIS MOTORS LIMITED, COWLEY, OXFORD

London Distributors: Morris House, Berkeley Square, W.1. Overseas Business: Nuffield Exports Limited, Oxford, & 41 Piccadilly, London, W.1.

C 295A (57)

ZIP

GOES A "1000"

From £455.0.0
(plus £228.17.0 P.T.)

THIS TRAVELLER REALLY TRAVELS

Always a brisk stepper, the newly-named Minor 1000 Traveller has been given a 20% power-boost. With its super-lively 950 c.c. O.H.V. engine, its roomy interior for passengers or cargo, this handy do-it-all is now more than ever 'the world's biggest buy' in multi-purpose motoring!

'QUALITY FIRST'
MORRIS *Minor 1000* TRAVELLER

Twelve Months' Warranty

MORRIS MOTORS LIMITED, COWLEY, OXFORD.
London Distributors: Morris House, Berkeley Square, W.1.
Overseas Business: Nuffield Exports Limited, Oxford & 41 Piccadilly, London, W.1.

At the time of these advertisements, in 1957, many prospective purchasers of the recently announced Morris 1000 would be accustomed to underpowered, small pre-war cars, (if they owned a car at all). The seemingly modest performance claims therefore would appear to be impressive in this context. The Morris Minor offered former users of public transport emancipation from bus and railway timetables.

journeys fell from 16,623 million in 1951 to 9,154 million by 1970. The closure of numerous railway and bus services affected many people, especially those in rural areas. Travelling became more difficult for many people - housewives, old and young people, those who could not afford to buy cars and others who were unable to drive. As Barker and Savage have commented, the "lot of those without access to cars undoubtedly grew worse." Faced with losses of passenger traffic to the private car from the 1950s, public bus and rail services had to be cut.

The table on the previous page shows the changing pattern of demand,

The Secret Life of the Morris Minor

and the percentage shares of different modes in total passenger mileage in Britain, 1952-69.

Obviously the Morris Minor, as the first British car to sell a million, played a large part (along with other popular car models of this era), in helping to cause the demise of public transport during this particular period. As we have seen, when faced with increasing competition from the private car, both railway and bus services had to react to changing economic conditions and cutbacks had to be made. It is possibly more difficult for motorists today, looking back from the crowded roads of the 1990s (with their often seemingly endless traffic jams), to appreciate exactly what the Morris Minor and other cars offered ordinary people in the late Forties and throughout the 1950s. Above all, it offered something that public transport could not compete with - freedom and independence. You could go out for a drive into the country or to the seaside, and return when you wanted to. It is hardly surprising, then, that the private car has become as popular as it has done.

The following figures illustrate the changing pattern of British consumers' expenditure on transport -

Percentage of consumers' expenditure		
Year	Public transport	Private motoring
1953	3.9	3.3
1958	3.4	3.8
1965	3.2	7.3
1971	3.3	9.4

(Source: Barker and Savage, 1974).

The Morris Minor provides employment

The Morris Minor provided employment for many thousands of people throughout its long production run. It was assembled in a labour intensive manner, effectively by hand, and was checked by forty nine different inspectors during the assembly process.

Nuffield organisation publicity booklets inform us that 21,500 people were employed by the organisation in February 1950, rising to 23,000 by August 1952. The factory grouping of the Nuffield organisation in February 1950 was as follows -

Group I
Foundries at Coventry and Wellingborough; engines factories at Courthouse Green and the old Riley Works; Nuffield Tools and Gauges; S.U. Carburetter Company; Tractor and Transmissions Branch at the Birmingham Wolseley Works.

Group II
Nuffield Exports Limited; Nuffield (Australia) Pty. Limited; Nuffield House, Piccadilly.

Group III
Cars Branch, Cowley (Morris and Wolseley cars and Morris vans); Riley and M.G. at Abingdon; Bodies Branch at Coventry; Morris Commercial Cars Limited, Birmingham.

Group IV
Nuffield Metal Products, Birmingham; radiators and pressings branches at North Oxford and at Llanelly.

(Source: Nuffield Organisation A Great Industrial Achievement, *1950).*

The Secret Life of the Morris Minor

Above: How Morris made the Minor! A view of the Number 4 Cowley assembly line in the early 1950s, showing the large number of people needed to manufacture the car.

Left: No automation to be seen here. The unloading end of the car body dipping plant typifies the labour intensity of the Minor's manufacture. Three (or possibly four) people pushing and three watching!

The Secret Life of the Morris Minor

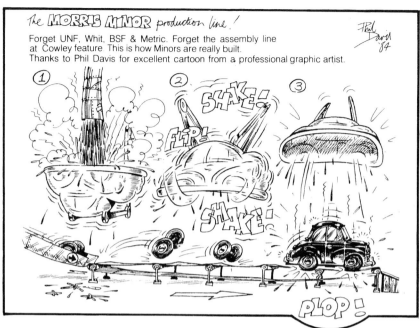

The MORRIS MINOR production line!

Forget UNF, Whit, BSF & Metric. Forget the assembly line at Cowley feature. This is how Minors are really built.
Thanks to Phil Davis for excellent cartoon from a professional graphic artist.

This cartoon from Minor Matters *shows how Minors were really made!*

BMC employed about 82,000 workers by 1963, with major assembly plants at Cowley, Longbridge and Abingdon. The British Leyland group employed over 180,000 workers by 1970. Data is not available for the number of workers involved in the manufacture of any one particular model of motor car. However, a substantial number of people included in these figures must have been involved in the manufacture of the Morris Minor. These figures include office workers and engineers, as well as assembly line workers.

During the early years of production, demand for the new Minor far exceeded supply. The waiting list for "the Minor Thousand was three months long" according to *Autocar* magazine in 1957 and BMC had to introduce overtime working in order to cut the backlog. This meant a full five-day week with some overtime for many workers at Cowley. A visiting journalist commented that the new Morris Minor had "captured the public imagination in a way that happens only rarely," and that its latest version, the Morris 1000, seemed in 1957 "likely to prolong the life of the design to a span of years that might rival those of the Model T." In fact, the Minor design - from the Series MM version in 1948, to the final version of the car, the Minor 1000 - was actually produced for more years than the Model T Ford. Minor assembly line workers at Cowley were amongst the newly affluent workers from the late 1950s, earning high wages. British car workers increased their pay by over 160 per cent between 1948 and 1964 compared with 140 per cent in engineering as a whole.

The Morris Minor was also assembled abroad in Australia, New Zealand, Eire, the Netherlands, India, South Africa and Denmark (the plant at Amersfoort in Holland produced 20,000 Minors by 1958). These "CKD" models (meaning Completely Knocked Down) were shipped in packing cases to places abroad, where they were assembled. Local suppliers were used for parts like tyres, batteries, paint, glass, interior fittings and upholstery. This form of export allowed the Nuffield organisation to avoid the high tariffs on imported cars in some markets - Andrews and Brunner quote a figure of £90 tariff on each car imported into Australia from the UK in about 1945. Thus, the Minor provided employment for many people abroad, as well as at home.

There were also many people employed by suppliers who produced parts for the Morris Minor. Turner has noted that BMC had 4000 different suppliers in 1963. Other suppliers after the Morris Minors were sold include spare parts dealers, petrol stations and providers of garage services.

Excluding items such as minor trim parts, wires, bolts, nuts, and so on, the major suppliers of parts for the Morris Minor were as follows -

The Morris Minor provides employment

PART	SUPPLIER
Complete bodyshell	Nuffield Metal Products, Birmingham.
Engine & gearbox	BMC, Longbridge.
Front suspension links & torsion bars	Morris Motors Tractors & Transmissions Branch.
Radiator	Morris Radiators Ltd, Oxford.
Steering gear & rear axle	Morris Motors Tractors & Transmissions Branch.
Universal joints & propeller shaft	Hardy Spicer Ltd, Birmingham.
Braking system	Lockheed Hydraulic Brake Co. Ltd, Leamington Spa.
Electrical system	Joseph Lucas Ltd, Birmingham.
Spring dampers	Armstrong Patents Ltd, Beverley.
Rear springs	English Steel Spring Corporation Ltd, Sheffield (& others).
Wheels	Dunlop Rim and Wheel Co. Ltd, Coventry.
Tyres	Dunlop Rubber Co. Ltd, Birmingham.
Bumpers	The Pyrene Co. Ltd, Brentford.
Steering wheels	Bluemel Bros. Ltd, Coventry & Wilmot-Breeden Ltd, Birmingham.
Instruments	S. Smith & Sons Ltd, London.
Leather	Connolly Bros. (Curriers) Ltd, London.
Vynide	I.C.I. (Hyde) Ltd, Hyde.
Carpets	John Crossley & Sons Ltd, Halifax.

(*Source:* Thoroughbred & Classic Cars, *June 1988*).

With these major parts and many minor items (totalling over 20,000 pieces altogether in each car), the assembly process could take place.

Who bought the Morris Minor?

The Morris Minor was treated as being just one model in a range of cars and was never heavily promoted by successive sales departments. The Cowley sales department felt that the Morris Oxford (a medium-sized family saloon) "would far outsell the Minor." Early advertisements and sales brochures thus placed the Minor behind the Oxford. In the event, the Minor outsold the Morris Oxford by almost two to one between 1948 and 1954; 159,960 of all Oxford types were built, according to Robson. This is far less than the total number of Minors produced.

The Morris Oxford and Morris Six models, whilst being visually similar to the Minor, were never as successful as the smaller car. The proportions of these models look somehow more bulbous when compared with those of the Minor and they appear narrower than the Minor in relation to their length. Scaled up, the Minor design seems less attractive. The Oxford was a "stolid vehicle" - its "compound curves were less pleasing" than the Minor's, according to Sedgwick. It had a 4-cylinder, 1.5-litre sidevalve engine (giving 41bhp), a disappointing steering column gearchange and a top speed of 71mph. It had a unitary body-chassis structure, like the Minor. It was, as Robson has noted, "an unexciting car" with "a stodgy performance and character which could not match the chassis." However, as an underpowered heavy car with a vague gear-change, it was possibly no worse than many of its contemporaries. The Morris Six used the Oxford's unitary chassis-body structure. It could outperform most of its contemporary rivals, with its top speed of over 80mph. It had a six-cylinder, single ohc engine of 2215cc. The Morris Six had a long bonnet and traditional upright grille - and was therefore more to Lord Nuffield's personal taste than the Minor. However, as Sedgwick notes, its "engine was difficult to service, the long bonnet impeded vision and handling was poor." The Morris Six did not sell very well - only about 12,400 of these cars had been made by 1954, when production ceased

Lord Nuffield's dislike of the Morris Minor has already been mentioned

Who bought the Morris Minor?

Who bought the Morris Minor?

These pictures, reproduced from 8hp Series E brochures, illustrate how the Minor followed an established theme in cultivating an upper middle-class image. Did Series E owners really live in the stockbroker belt, or are these merely the poor relations seeing how the other half lives?

The Secret Life of the Morris Minor

but, at the official launch of the Minor in 1948, he "refused even to drive the new car for publicity purposes." This seems to have been a strange attitude for the chairman of any company to adopt, (especially the chairman of a vast company like the Nuffield organisation) towards one of the products it was trying to sell!

Some early Morris Minor sales brochures use quotations from the motoring press and others praising the car - though these were very conservatively placed on the back of the brochures. In the 1953 "Quality First" sales brochure, a *Sunday Express* newspaper quote from Stirling Moss was used to endorse the Morris Minor. Moss said "I approved the Minor's superb handling qualities, near-perfect steering, first-class suspension and rugged character under stress. In a phrase, the world's best baby car." This was praise indeed, coming from one of Britain's top racing drivers.

The exception to the rule of selling the Minor as part of a range of cars were the 350 "Minor Million" limited edition cars produced in 1960. These were two-door saloons with special features such as lilac paint, off-white upholstery and special Morris "1,000,000" bonnet and boot badges. The colour of these cars, whilst being distinctive, was not entirely to everyone's taste. These particular cars were used by BMC dealers to create publicity for the Morris Minor. Alec Issigonis presented the actual millionth Minor produced to the National Union of Journalists who used it to raise funds for charity.

Sales figures do not indicate the class, sex and age of purchasers. However, early brochures featured well-dressed, middle-class families who played tennis and golf - following on from Morris Eight Series E advertising. Most early Minor buyers would have been middle-class people. However, from the late Fifties onwards, many manual workers could afford to buy used cars including Morris Minors. The following table shows the proportion of households and persons in those households owning cars in England and Wales, by social class, in 1966 (percentages) -

| | NO CAR | | ONE OR MORE CARS | |
	HOUSEHOLDS	PERSONS	HOUSEHOLDS	PERSONS
Social class				
Professional, managerial & intermediate non-manual	25.0	20.8	75.0	79.3
Junior non-manual & personal service	57.3	50.2	42.7	49.9
Skilled manual	51.3	49.3	48.7	50.6
Semi-skilled & unskilled manual	73.5	70.2	26.5	29.8
All classes	50.8	46.9	49.2	53.1

(Source: Halsey, 1972).

Early postwar Morris Motors publicity material placed emphasis on the mid-range Series MO Oxford. The Morris Oxford was expected to have the widest appeal in sales terms.

This advert shows a global approach to marketing, probably as a result of the "export or die" policy imposed by the postwar British government. Over 75 per cent of early Morris Minors were exported.

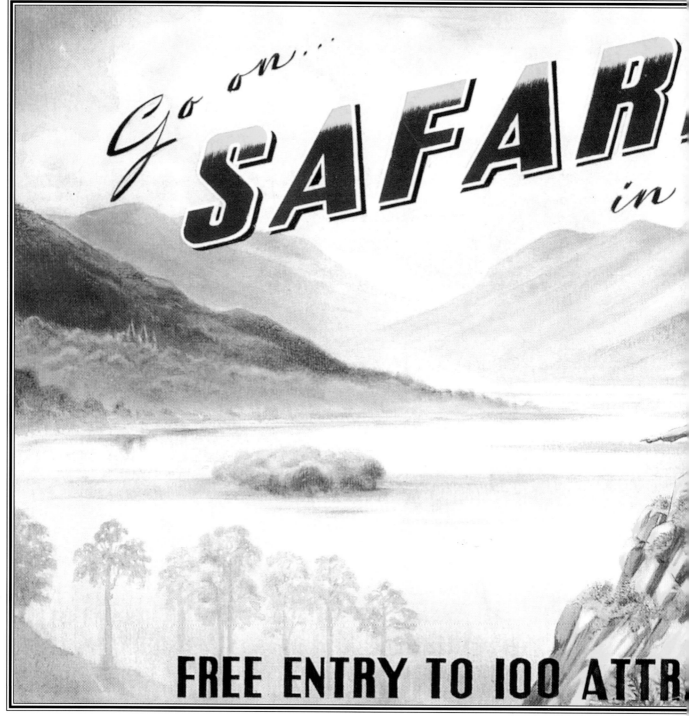

Shell's 1991 Explore Britain Promotion featured a number of British classic cars, all of which were sports models apart from the Morris Minor Traveller shown here.

The Secret Life of the Morris Minor

This 1950 sales brochure centrefold shows how the Minor complimented a range of larger cars (unlike the VW Beetle) and therefore had to share its maker's resources with these other cars.

Left & facing page, top: With its eye-catching lilac paintwork, ivory interior and Minor 1,000,000 badges, the "Minor Million" represents two firsts for the British motor industry - one, the Morris Minor was the first British vehicle to exceed the total of 1 million units produced and, two, the 350 Minor Million cars were the first limited edition models to be marketed by a British car manufacturer.

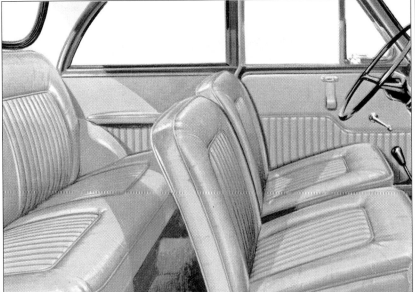

Below: This sales brochure illustration accentuates the interior roominess of the late Series II convertible.

Sales brochure from the later years of Minor production showing the final revision of the car's interior. The Austin-inspired front seats lacked the comfort of earlier Minor seats.

The Secret Life of the Morris Minor

Above: This illustration from a 1955 sales brochure emphasizes the low running costs and value for money offered by the late Series II Minor saloon, virtues that would be appreciated during the upcoming Suez crisis.

Right: Early sales brochures for the Morris Minor tended to show it as a vehicle owned by reasonably prosperous families

In a class of its own
for "Quality First" Features

Look where you will on the roads of the world and there you will see "Quality First"

Morris cars road-proving their reliability. They have created a new and higher class of their own,

excelling in performance and comfortable travel. No wonder Nuffield's were the first

European manufacturers to build 2,000,000 vehicles.

The "Quality First"
MORRIS

MORRIS MOTORS LIMITED COWLEY, OXFORD. OVERSEAS BUSINESS: NUFFIELD EXPORTS LIMITED, OXFORD, AND 41 PICCADILLY, LONDON.

Publicity material frequently showed women in the driving seat of the Morris Minor throughout the era of its production

Besides the public utilities, the largest purchaser of Minor LCVs was the Post Office, a long established Morris customer. Pictured above is a Series II telephone engineer's van embodying special features, built in at the request of the Post Office, such as the ladder rack, opening driver's windscreen and rubber front wings with separate headlamps in a raised position (were these engineers especially accident prone drivers?) Below is a late Royal Mail delivery van whose special features were mainly confined to the vehicle interior and the provision of high security door locks.

The Secret Life of the Morris Minor

Above: The Minor was advertised as being ideal for both business and pleasure use and early brochures frequently depicted left-hand drive cars, thus emphasizing the importance of the export market.

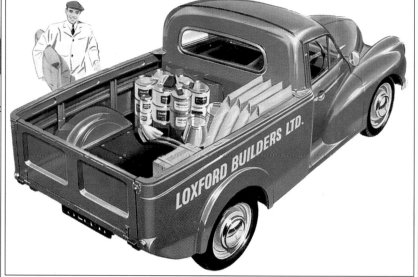

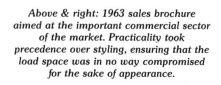

Above & right: 1963 sales brochure aimed at the important commercial sector of the market. Practicality took precedence over styling, ensuring that the load space was in no way compromised for the sake of appearance.

For people with an eye for a bargain
The Morris Minor 1000 Traveller...

The manufacturers never attempted to endow the Minor with a supposed youth image, as this illustration from a late brochure would testify. It would appear from this picture that antiques dealers were attracted to the car years before the BBC Lovejoy series was made!

Since the early days of production the Minor has been totally 'classless,' owned by manual and non-manual workers, famous and ordinary people alike. Past Morris Minor owners have included television and pop stars, Members of Parliament and several Archbishops of Canterbury. Many sales brochures show women driving the cars. Although statistics show low levels of car purchase by women, these figures hide the many women whose husbands bought a Minor for them as a second family car. The table overleaf shows the proportion of the British population with one or more cars in 1949 by sex and social class (percentages).

The Secret Life of the Morris Minor

	ALL CLASSES	AB	C	DE
Men	13.1	46.8	21.2	5.6
Women	2.1	8.8	3.1	0.8
Total men & women	7.2	26.5	11.5	3.0

Owners of one or more cars, 1949 (*Source: Halsey, 1972*).

1960s period publicity photograph of a Morris Traveller, fairly typical of BMC material at this time. The half-timbered styling of the car blends in well with the rustic surroundings.

With regard to the age of owners, married women with families and older people were usually featured in advertisements or publicity material (though there were a few exceptions to this rule, in later BMC material, for example). This seems generally to have reflected the buyers of the Minor - teenagers were shown with newer BMC models. However, in recent years, young people have increasingly bought Minors, either for cheap transportation or as 'classic' cars. Others have modified their Minors, and made them more powerful (by putting in MG Midget engines or twin ohc Fiat engines, for example).

The Morris Minor light commercial vehicles catered for the important business sector. Buyers included the GPO (Royal Mail) - following on from

Rear view of pick-up showing optional tilt cover enclosing load area.

Who bought the Morris Minor?

Latin heart transplant. The Fiat twin ohc engine and associated 5-speed gearbox have become a popular way of giving a huge power boost to the Morris Minor.

their purchase of Morris E Series Z vans, Post Office Telephones and government departments, as well as numerous other firms in Britain and abroad. Some Minor CVs appeared as Austins during the late Leyland period (1968 onwards) with special Austin badges and crinkled grilles, in order to meet Austin dealers' demands.

Above: Unlike the passenger cars, light commercial vehicles had separate chassis frames, thus enabling buyers to have bodywork to suit their specific requirements; e.g, gown vans.

Owing to the foolish segregation of Morris and Austin franchises, to enable the latter to sell new Minor LCVs they were fitted with badges and grilles to identify them as Austins. This satisfied the dealers and fooled no one else!

Production ends

After the merger of BMC into the newly-formed British Leyland group in 1968, the decision was taken to gradually phase out the Morris Minor. There were a number of reasons for this. Firstly, demand had fallen off throughout the 1960s, and sales had declined steadily. The cars had become uneconomic to produce, being assembled in three different locations in Britain (Birmingham, Coventry and Cowley) and using out-dated, and labour-intensive manufacturing techniques (the Traveller, for example, contained about fifty separate pieces of wood).

The following schedule shows the length of time taken for the various assembly operations on the production line -

a) 3 hours
Arrival of bodyshell in Preparation Department. Fit rear spring brackets; underseal seams; fit door locks remote control mechanism; allocate body numbers and slave equipment; spray floor and boot with anti-drum material.

b) 2.5 hours
General Inspection. Face-off primer and stop; face-off stopper; spray filler; wet sand primer; dry off, spirit wipe; spray sealer; stop and dry sand; inspect and rectify; spray colour.

c) 2 hours
Body to baking oven. Touch-up and paint battery shelf.

d) 1 hour
Arrival on assembly line. Fit rear axle; install engine and gearbox; mount front suspension; fit all electrical equipment; fit windscreen, rear light and side windows; trim interior. Inspect and rectify.

Late Morris advertisement. Can one believe the claims that a Minor was sold every ten minutes in the knowledge that production was running down by this time? (Does this car's registration number refer to the dreaded axle tramp?

e) 30 minutes
Arrival on assembly line. Extensive inspection and rectification; check headlamps; place car on rollers and tune engine; despatch car to delivery bay with notes for other work needed.

(*Source*: Thoroughbred & Classic Cars, *June 1988*).

Profitability of BMC cars was low when compared with other companies,

The Secret Life of the Morris Minor

Inserting the power unit with a hoist at the factory - homespun methods reminiscent of a Minor owner repairing the car in his garage at home.

Adjusting the door striker plate - add the wheels and this could be any suburban drive rather than the factory.

MORRIS can take it...

Whatever your needs there is a car in the new Morris range to suit you. Morris is the name for family motoring. From the exhilarating Mini Mk. II (with its new 998-c.c. engine) and the new 1300, to the luxurious and powerful 1800, there is a car sized, powered and priced to meet your exact requirements. Choose the car that suits you, whether a saloon, traveller or convertible, and enjoy the best of everything with comfort, economy, and lively performance. Whatever your family needs, it needs a MORRIS.

so—make it a **MORRIS**

The front cover of the 1967 Morris Can Take It brochure. By the 1960s, the Minor looked decidedly old-fashioned when compared with newer BMC models, but it continued to sell despite being relegated to the background by the publicity department - as illustrated here.

such as Ford for example. By 1968 the return on each Morris Minor sold was only about £9. Thus, in view of the falling numbers of Minors being sold, the car was actually losing money from British Leyland's point of view. However, BMC engineers felt that the car could "easily have become Britain's answer to the Volkswagen Beetle" if its marketing and "development had not been neglected" according to Turner. (In the 1950s, Issigonis had a front-wheel drive Minor prototype running, but this had not been developed further by BMC). The Morris Minor's lack of development contributed to its declining sales during the 1960s. A more powerful engine for the car was needed, especially in certain overseas markets such as the USA.

The Morris Minor was generally perceived as being old-fashioned and cramped by the early 1960s, by both public and motoring press alike. Its rounded style looked outdated when compared with the boxy shape of more recent models, such as the Triumph Herald, BMC Mini, Ford Anglia (105E) and the Farina styled Austin A40. The Minor, which had looked so modern in 1948, looked decidedly old fashioned 21 years later. It was also slower than most of its competitors by this time (see appendix 2). More modern front-wheel-drive cars, such as the BMC 1100/1300, offered features like all-round independent suspension and had much greater interior space than the Minor. Shortly after the car finished its production run in 1971, it was described by *Motor* magazine as "the favourite car of district nurses and retired old gentlemen who do not hold with the new-fangled front-wheel-drive." This staid image evidently contributed towards the decline in sales of the car throughout the 1960s.

The Leyland management decided to replace the Morris Minor with the larger, more modern-looking Marina models in two different engine sizes - 1300cc and 1800cc - to compete directly with the Ford Escort/Cortina and Vauxhall Viva/Victor. The small car market sector was declining at this time. As Sedgwick commented succinctly, the Morris Minor was "killed off to make room for the uninspired Marina." The Morris Marina was designed by a committee and, unlike the Minor, was not the imaginative creation of one man's fertile mind. It is ironic that the Marina failed to outsell its predecessor.

Although sharing the same suspension layout as the Minor, most of the Marina's components were different from those used on the earlier car. One of the Minor's less desirable features - axle tramp when accelerating sharply - showed up on the Morris Marina too. The Marina lacked the excellent handling qualities of the Minor - its steering was less precise and did not respond as readily as the Minor's steering. However, the wider wheels and radial tyres used on the Marina gave it better roadholding than the Minor. More to the point, the Minor was much more enjoyable to drive. The Marina suffered from ferocious clutch judder, possibly as a result of the deletion of the engine steady bar which was a feature of the Minor.

When the various types of Minor were phased out (see appendix 4) there was little mention in the press. In Oxford, where the car had provided employment for over twenty years, the production of the last Minor saloon was referred to in passing in a leading article about wage agreements and labour relations at the Cowley factory. When the last Traveller was produced, in 1971, an "era had ended" according to Michael Sedgwick.

The Morris Minor
and the Environment

Since the late 1950s and early 1960s, the "recent expansion of the environmental movement" has taken place, according to Lowe and Goyder. This period of time saw the huge growth of interest in environmental issues and the formation of many environmental pressure groups, including the Council for Nature, the Noise Abatement Society and the British Trust for Conservation Volunteers. Environmental conservation has rocketed from obscurity to a position of world influence, greatly helped by the media. The British Department of the Environment was set up in 1970, in response to particular environmental issues.

Events such as the Torrey Canyon oilspill off Britain's Cornish coast and the mass poisoning of fish in Germany's river Rhine aroused public concern. In March 1967 the Torrey Canyon, a 118,000 ton oil tanker, hit rocks off the Scilly Isles. Almost 25,000 tons of oil drifted ashore before the winds changed direction. The oilspill had a devastating effect on the wildlife in the area: badly oiled guillemots were just some of the numerous birds who were victims of the pollution. About 5000 people were needed to clean up the damage. Costs were in the region of £10 million, not including the losses to the local tourist trade.

The energy crisis of 1973 and the ensuing oil shortage drew public attention to the fact that oil was not an infinite resource. Since that time, the environmental movement has experienced dramatic growth, with the formation of many new pressure groups such as the Friends of the Earth, the Ecology Party and Transport 2000.

Recent research has highlighted several environmental problems caused partly by motor vehicles. Lead in petrol, for example, has been linked with brain damage to young children. The emission of carbon dioxide has been linked with global warming (the "greenhouse effect"). Other by-products of internal combustion, such as nitrogen oxides, have been shown to cause smog and acid rain. "Acid rain" has been linked with damage to, and the death of

The Secret Life of the Morris Minor

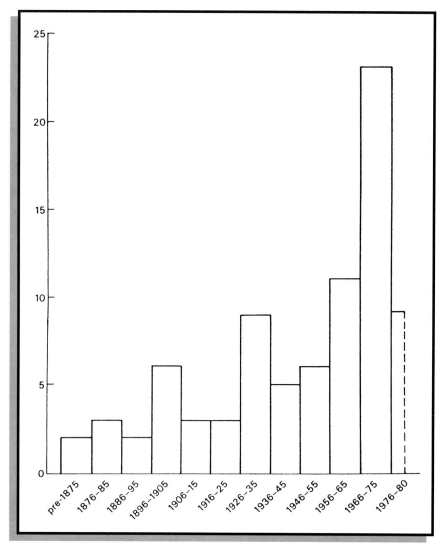

This graph dramatically demonstrates the increasing awareness of environmental issues, and shows the formation of relevant pressure groups in the UK up to 1980. (From Environmental Groups In Politics, by P Lowe & J Goyder, Allen & Unwin)

forests as well as the killing of fish in lakes. This phenomenon is known to be caused by the discharge of certain toxic chemicals, including nitrogen oxides, into the atmosphere - some the by-products of the internal combustion engine. EEC legislation has meant that, from October 1990, all new cars sold in member states have to be able to run on unleaded petrol and, from the end of 1992, all new cars had to be equipped with catalytic converters.

Although not built since 1971, the Morris Minor has also benefited from recent developments aimed at reducing automotive pollution. In response to public demand, spare parts manufacturers have supplied items since early 1989 to turn the car into a 'green' vehicle. It has become possible to purchase a replacement cylinder head with special valve seats and valves which enables the Minor to run on unleaded petrol. It is possible to obtain a catalytic converter for the car too. Thus, it is already possible to modify the Minor into a more environmentally friendly car and further developments are likely in the future.

In recent years, letters to *Minor Matters* (the magazine produced by the Morris Minor Owners Club) have reflected the desire of many Morris Minor owners to make their cars more environmentally friendly. There has been a flood of letters to the *Technical Tips* section of the magazine regarding running Minors on unleaded fuel.

It is more environmentally friendly to purchase an existing car, such as a Morris Minor, and keep it for many years instead of purchasing a new car every three years or so. Modern car factories and the plants that turn scrapped cars back into steel are vast consumers of energy. Having said this, the Morris Minor centre has been developing a new factory in Sri Lanka which will hand-build new Minors. Part of the philosophy behind this operation is environmental; over 95 per cent of tasks involved in building the cars being carried out by hand and few power tools being used. Manually powered hydraulic presses will be used. It is hoped that complete new Morris Minors (both left-hand and right-hand-drive models) will be manufactured in Sri Lanka and the Morris Minor Centre plans to build about 3000 new Minors a year. In July 1991 the company had fifty employees in Sri Lanka and hoped to be employing about

The Morris Minor & the Environment

Typical example of rotten and filled timber framing on a Morris Traveller, (a potential MoT failure for these cars). Ash, being a fast growing tree, is a readily renewable resource.

one thousand local people within four years thus providing work for many people in Batadua, a region of high unemployment.

As a last thought on environmentally sound materials, the Traveller body frame, being ash, is readily renewable because the ash tree grows quickly (the Common Ash can soon attain heights of 60 feet, and over, and does well in virtually any soil or situation).

Rotten wood on Minor Travellers is renowned - it featured in this Daily Mail "Yuppies" cartoon strip.

Enduring popularity

British society has always had a strong tradition of historicism - that is, of looking back fondly to past eras. However, since the late 1960s, there has been a general growth in nostalgia throughout British society. Perhaps the most overt evidence of this phenomenon has been the huge amount of public debate on modern versus classical architecture in 1990s Britain: as a consequence many people have rejected the aims of the modernist movement. British design in general has also reflected a trend to re-embrace traditional values. Sparke commented recently that "the dominant styles of the day are nostalgic and revivalist."

The growth of interest in the past can be seen by the desire of many people to preserve former modes of everyday transportation. The last British Rail steam locomotives ran in 1968 but, since this time, a huge number of private railway societies have been formed and locomotives preserved or restored. A 1990 British Coal *Guide to Steam Trains* listed over 120 steam centres in Britain, most of which ran live steam. Three of the best-known of these are the Didcot Railway Centre, the Severn Valley Railway and the Bluebell Line.

The classic car movement has also grown enormously in recent years, along with the number of car clubs and magazines devoted to the subject (in this context the term 'classic car' refers to any cherished older car). Classic car owners have been increasingly recognised by the media. A number of cartoons in national newspapers, for example, have looked humorously at the classic car enthusiast - including the Morris Minor owner. Cartoons have tended to depict classic car owners as slightly eccentric figures who sentimentally cosset their vehicles and live in the past (whilst occasionally raiding scrapyards for some treasured part or other)! In general, the classic car owner has usually been seen as a harmless but nice person, and the humour is usually all in good part. After all, the reason many classic car owners buy their vehicles in the first place is that they want to be different from everyone else: not everyone wants to drive around in an anonymous modern hatchback. Like me, many of you

"WHEN BUYING A MINOR, IT'S BEST TO GO FOR THE 'ALL ORIGINAL, ONE ELDERLY OWNER' EXAMPLES..."

will be quite good at identifying most models of car over about ten years of age but have to examine closely the name badges of modern cars to find out exactly which manufacturer made them - let alone which particular model they are.

The Morris Minor Owners Club is one of the largest classic car clubs with over 10,000 members at the present time. It caters for all Minors produced between 1948 and 1971, including the 'Austin' Minor commercial vehicles. Club members receive an excellent magazine, *Minor Matters*, every two months - this gives them information about spares, technical advice and so on. The club also arranges rallies for members and holds many local regional meetings, so that Minor owners can meet socially. An overseas trip is undertaken by more adventurous Minor owners (and healthier Minors) once a year. There are many benefits for club members including discounts on spares sold by some suppliers, a special insurance scheme and discounted RAC membership. For further information write, enclosing an SAE, to - Jane White, Membership Secretary, 127-129 Green Lane, Derby DE1 1RZ

The Morris Minor has often featured in British popular culture - in poems and songs for example. Songs have tended to concentrate, not surprisingly,

This cartoon sends up the classic car movement and was done by a Morris enthusiast after Charles Ware of the Morris Minor Centre described how he had been conned by an old lady in Norfolk, whose botching sons used her as a selling 'front'. (Copyright of the Morris Minor Centre)

The Secret Life of the Morris Minor

This picture came from a book of paintings by James Grainger entitled Vicarage Allsorts - it conjures up an image which springs to mind at the mention of the words "Morris Dancing"!

on the car's legendary reliability and its lasting qualities -

Morris Minor
Never lets you down
Gets you round the town
Straight from A to B
Nothing finer
I don't need to dash
Or to be dead flash
So that's the car for me

I don't need the rest
'Cause I'm happy with the best
So that's the car for me

("The Morris Minor Song," sung by Morris Minor and the Majors)

Got myself a Morris Minor 1963
May not be a Roller but its good enough for me
You can say it may not be the

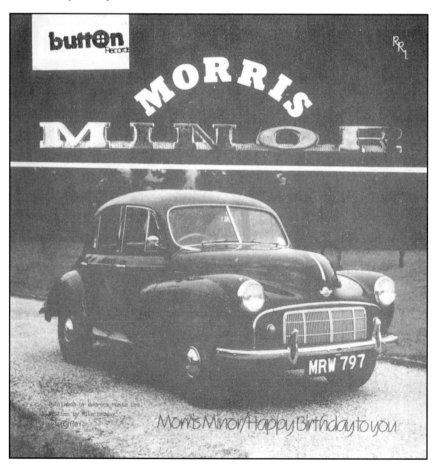

The record cover of Morris Minor by Mike Redway featured a 4-door Series MM saloon.

70

Best set of wheels you've ever seen

Morris Minor
Styled like an ocean liner
Always a pleasure to see
Morris Minor
Always a joy to shine her
Oh, such a treasure to me
While there'll be laughter
You'll be here long after
Other motor cars have ceased to be

Ten wild horses in a line-up
Taking me in style
May not burn up rubber
But there's fun in every mile
Fun and laughter all the way and
We may not be back home for tea
But when we go
We sure do go
My Minor dynamo and me

("Morris Minor," sung by Mike Redway, published by Redrock Music)

In the same way, a poem by popular poetess, Pam Ayres, refers to the Minor's reliability - how it took her over ninety thousand miles without letting her down. She also shows great affection for her first car and gives it human qualities - referring to the headlamps as eyes, for example. The way in which she describes the demise of this vehicle, (turning rusty and, unfortunately, going to the scrapyard) is like describing the passing of an old friend -

Oh love, you got no poke left
I didn't want to say
It seems we are outmoded,
Much too slow, and in the way
You know how much I love you
I'd repair you in a flash
But I haven't got the knowledge
And I haven't got the cash.

There is rust all round your headlamps
I could push through if I tried
My pot of paint can't cure it
'Cause it's from the other side.
All along your sides and middle
You are turning rusty brown
Though you took me ninety thousand miles
And never let me down.

Not the snapping of a fan belt
Nor the blowing of a tyre

The Secret Life of the Morris Minor

Pam Ayres's poem says it all!

BBC TV programme, **Some Mothers Do** **Ave Em.** *In the episode entitled* **Oh I Do** **Like To Be Beside The Seaside,** *Frank Spencer (Michael Crawford) finds an unusual place to park during a trip to the sea. At this point, he is hanging from the Morris Minor's tailpipe over the edge of a cliff!* (Copyright © BBC).

Nor the rattling of a tappet
And nor did you misfire.
All your wheels stayed on the corners
And your wipers on the screen
Though I didn't do much for you
And I never kept you clean.

All your seats are unupholstered
And foam rubber specks the floor,
You were hit by something else once
And I cannot shut the door
But it's not those things that grieve me
Or the money that I spent
For you were my first-driven,
Ninety thousand miles we went.
I could buy a bright new car
And go tearing round the town
A BGT! A Morgan!
(With the hood all battened down).
But as I leave you in the scrapyard,
Bangers piled up to the skies,
Why do your rusty headlamps
Look like sad, reproachful eyes?

("Good-bye Worn Out Morris 1000," by Pam Ayres).

As well in featuring in popular British poems and songs, the Morris Minor frequently appears in films and also on television, the dominant transmitter of popular culture. As Shannon has noted (writing in the *Sunday Telegraph Magazine* in 1986), first of all the Minor was just used as an example of what ordinary people drove; later, it became more of a joke car.

The Minor has been particularly popular in comedy series. In one memorable episode of the TV comedy *Some Mothers Do 'Ave 'Em*, Frank Spencer (played by Michael Crawford) ended up holding on to the tailpipe of a Minor as it balanced precariously on the edge of a cliff. Other comedy TV programmes in which the Minor has appeared include *Sorry* (starring Ronnie Corbett), *The Dick Emery Show* (when Dick Emery, on one occasion, reversed a Minor into a river) and *Open All Hours* (starring Ronnie Barker, David Jason and Linda Baron). In *Open All Hours*, a white Minor saloon is driven by Nurse Gladys Emmanuel and, in one particular episode, Arkwright's trousers were hanging from the roof rack of the Minor: said trousers eventually coming off and landing in the face of a motorcyclist. A Trafalgar Blue convertible appears in the BBC TV comedy-drama series *Lovejoy*. This particular Minor, known as "Miriam," seems to have started a new lease of life. In the last series it looked decidedly neglected, since when it has been restored and is slightly customised with a small, sports-type steering wheel, wide pressed steel wheels and a non-standard sounding engine.

The Minor has also appeared in more serious TV drama programmes such as *The Chinese Detective* and the *Miss Marple* series. In *Howard's Way* (where a green Traveller appeared as the only 'ordinary' car (that is, compared to the Bentley, Saab Turbo and Jaguar which also appeared) and the Minor was

This 1980s Stork Margarine poster is a comic illustration which shows the Morris Minor as an accepted part of the British way of life.

A still from a Shell Oil television commercial featuring the incongruous sight of a Minor convertible apparently competing in a Grand Prix race. Not quite what you would expect Mansell or Hill to be driving but BBC motor racing commentator Murray Walker did have one!

shown as either forever breaking down or being worked upon - a somewhat annoying image for Minor owners who appreciate the car's reliability.

The Minor has featured in many advertisements too, including those used by British Gas and the Milk Marketing Board. In a Shell advertisement, a white Minor convertible was seen driving into the pit stop of a racing track. having its windows wiped and wheels changed and driving off again! A National West-

The Secret Life of the Morris Minor

This cartoon from the Observer Magazine depicts a slightly eccentric Minor owner pampering his car. His affection is bestowed upon a visibly humanoid Minor saloon. (Courtesy Ken Taylor and The Observer © copyright The Observer, London 1986).

minster Bank commercial which showed a Minor disintegrating outside one of its branches was not appreciated by most Minor owners, who boast about the car's durability. A Stork SB Margarine poster was seen on hoardings all over the country. Entitled "The Great British Picnic," it showed a cartoon family having a picnic. The Minor saloon in the cartoon was well drawn and detailed.

The Morris Minor has been noted for the affection it has inspired in many of its owners. Like those of the earlier Model T Ford, owners have tended to give their Minor a name - usually female - and treated it like a pet or member of the family. "Doris" seems to be a particularly popular name but, so too, are other rhyming names such as "Horace" and "Maurice." (My own car has been given the highly unoriginal name of "Boris"). Other names are derived from the cars' numberplates. The reasons for psychological attachment to the Minor are various. The social scientist, Dr. Peter Marsh, ascribes this appeal partly to the car's "characteristic round shape," which he describes as being "reminiscent of a young animal." Another factor may be the essentially 'female' character of the car. Harley Earl, the General Motors designer, was noted for frequently referring to "parts of a car as resembling certain anatomical parts of the female," according to Armi. In a similar manner, Arkwright, in *Open All Hours* the BBC television comedy programme, imparted the Morris Minor with feminine qualities, saying that it reminded him of his fiancee, Nurse Gladys Emmanuel, being "curvy of bonnet and rounded of boot."

Postscript

To date, most of the published work on the subject of the Morris Minor has concentrated on purely descriptive history of the car itself. I have tried to examine the Morris Minor from different angles - for example, by looking at both American and European influences on the car's design in some detail. I have also researched and described the car's interrelationships with, and effects on British society since 1948 (in the wider context of social change during this period). I hope, thus, to have contributed some new knowledge to the history of design and technological developments since the 1930s and the ways in which the design processes themselves are affected by the demands of society.

The 1.2 million Minor production figure does not, of course, compare with over 15 million Volkswagen Beetles made by 1968. The Morris Minor had more interior space, was quieter than the air-cooled German car and had superior road holding qualities. The Volkswagen's swing-axle rear suspension was "particularly susceptible to sway in side winds," and could be dangerous under certain conditions, according to the *Motor* magazine in 1965. In many respects, the Morris Minor illustrates missed opportunity on the part of BMC, and graphically demonstrates the reasons why British manufacturing started to decline in world markets. The Beetle had better spares back up, and was more heavily advertised than the Minor. Export

The VW Beetle was a car intensely disliked by Alec Issigonis. It can be described as a triumph of workmanship over design. Pictured here is an early model.

The Secret Life of the Morris Minor

The Citroen 2CV. The car illustrated dates from the early 1970s when Citroen started marketing this model in Britain again in response to the energy crisis. This veritable "tent on wheels" contravenes most orthodox motoring values.

markets cried out for a bigger and more powerful engine for the Morris Minor, but BMC did not respond to this demand. As Adeney has commented, British car manufacturers were "always slow to think of customers' needs." Minors were exported to northern Scandinavia and other places where the weather was severely cold in winter without heaters, as they were not fitted as standard items: this attitude can be described as arrogance on the part of British manufacturers.

Apart from marketing, the main reason for the Minor's lack of success in America (where the Beetle was a huge success) can be summed up by one word, service! It was not easy for the American buyer of a Morris Minor to find reliable suppliers of spare parts and servicing for his or her car, and the availability of parts was much worse than for any American car. Also, American cars had very reliable electrical systems. The Minor suffered from the curse of most British cars of the time: Lucas electrics (systems referred to in the USA as having been made by "Joe Lucas Prince of Darkness"). It is believed by many BMC and British Leyland engineers that the British car, the Morris Minor could have outsold the German Beetle - if it had been given the right marketing, good spares back-up and some detail developments.

The Morris Minor has become one of the most ubiquitous of all British cars. The Minor 1000 neither looks nor sounds exactly the same as any other car. It is just as unique as two other small cars of roughly the same era, the Citroen 2CV and the Volkswagen Beetle. The Minor's distinctive features include a characteristic exhaust boom on the over-run, a noise which cannot be mistaken for that made by any other car.

A few years after production of the Minor ceased in 1971, a few individuals paid for new Morris Minors which would be assembled from brand new parts. This was surely testimony to the high regard in which the car was held by many people. These 'new' cars included a 2-door saloon built by the Dutton Forshaw Garage in Swindon for Rod Law, and a Snowberry White Traveller built by Jim Steed: front and rear bodyshells were provided by Appleyards of Leeds.

In many respects, the Morris Minor became the first "motor car for the masses" (a concept envisaged by William Morris early this century) by being the first British car to sell a million examples.

The Morris Minor was successfully rallied by many people. All the different types of Minor were good rally cars, apart from the Series II cars. Pat Moss, Stirling Moss' sister, drove a Morris Minor, number NMO 933 (and affectionately known as "Granny"), in many international rallies from 1957. The car "competed and finished well in just about every major international event," and was still being rallied four years later "long after other competition cars of its year had fallen to pieces or been pensioned off," according to Pat Moss . Possibly this car's best result was coming fourth overall in the 1958 RAC Rally

- thus taking first place in the 1000cc Touring Car Class and winning the Ladies' Cup for Pat Moss and Ann Wisdom (in dreadful weather conditions of snow and ice). Pat currently owns a green Minor 1000 convertible built in 1966.

In 1980, the Archbishop of Canterbury's Morris Minor (built in 1967) was entered in the first Himalayan Rally. The modifications made to this car were kept to a minimum. The Minor coped admirably with about 3000 miles of Indian roads - which included some of the highest mountain roads anywhere in the world. The car performed remarkably and suffered from few mechanical problems. It came 15th overall and won its class - beating many modern cars. As only half of the competitors finished (out of 75 starters), the Minor had survived "a remarkable journey" according to the entrant.

Morris Minors currently compete regularly in classic saloon car races. Stirling Moss praised the Morris Minor's handling qualities and owned one himself. His Minor was an early Series MM. However, Stirling Moss added a Derrington conversion to his Minor and this greatly improved the car's performance (giving it about 15 per cent more power than a standard Series MM Minor). In recent years, customisers have fitted all sorts of different engines to Morris Minors in order to obtain the ultimate in performance. Rover V8, Ford Cosworth and even huge 7.5-litre engines derived from American cars have been transferred to Morris Minor body shells. Some of these cars can reach speeds of over 150mph!

In 1956, *Motor* magazine remarked that "There has never been a bad Morris Minor" and that the car's "rugged reliability and ease of operation has endeared it to families all over the world." In 1958 the magazine also described the Morris Minor as Brit-

This picture shows the conditions endured during the first Himalayan Rally of 1980. A 13 year old Morris Minor (formerly the Archbishop of Canterbury's runabout) managed to finish the course successfully, competing against much more modern cars.

The good handling qualities of the Morris Minor endeared itself to enthusiastic drivers such as Stirling Moss, seen here in his modified Series MM. This picture, taken in 1950, also shows his sister Pat, who later became renowned as a BMC rally driver, competing in various cars including Morris Minor 1000s.

The Secret Life of the Morris Minor

THE MORRIS MINOR BRINGS BIG CAR MOTORING AT SMALL CAR COST

- Front seats upholstered in leather.
- Torsion bar independent front suspension.
- Hypoid final drive.
- Rack-and-pinion steering gearbox.
- Self-cancelling Trafficators.
- In-built demisting ducts.
- Provision for fitting heating and wireless.
- Four-speed synchromesh gearbox.
- Rustproofed " Mono-construction " body.
- Piston-type hydraulic shock absorbers at front and rear.
- Roof lamp.
- Main headlamp beam indicator in centre grille.

Above & facing page: Minor publicity material frequently featured pipe smokers - was the lavish provision of large ashtrays on the later cars connected with this?

ain's most successful postwar car.

I have been unable, in carrying out my research on the Morris Minor, to discover why such a small car needed so many and such large ashtrays! One wonders whether there is any correlation between the size and number of ashtrays on late Minors and the pipe smoking men so often shown in Morris sales brochures? (How many owners of Morris Minors have been pipe smokers, I wonder?)

The Morris Minor is a highly individual car model, which is full of character.

It has become one of the best-loved of all British car designs despite its few faults (such as the uncomfortable seats on late Minors, and the lack of power when compared with more modern vehicles). As we have seen, there are many reasons for the Minor's enduring appeal - and these have included social and economic factors. However, the psychological appeal of the car seems to be have been a particularly important factor in keeping so many Morris Minors on our roads in the 1990s, when most of its contemporaries (and many more modern cars since) have ended up in scrapyards. Many people have been attracted to the look of the car and want to drive one. The Morris Minor is practical to own and great fun to drive. As Pat Moss (now Carlsson) says, "If it's a very

good, reliable and economical little car you're looking for, then the Morris Minor is just for you."

In 1986 there were still an estimated 150,000 Morris Minors on British roads and with the support of enthusiasts and ordinary drivers alike, they are still a familiar sight today, not only in Britain but in a number of overseas countries such as Sri Lanka. The good news for all Morris Minor owners and would-be Minor owners is that the number of suppliers of parts for the car seems to be increasing continually. Hopefully, there will be many thousands of Morris Minors (no pun intended) used as everyday transport, both at home and abroad, until well into the next century.

In the words of Andrews and Brunner authors of *The Life of Lord Nuffield* (writing in 1955), the Morris Minor "has been phenomenally successful."

Appendix I
The Minor's Wolseley & Riley Sisters

The Riley 1.5. This car, together with the similar Wolseley 1500, had front suspension and steering assemblies derived from those of the Morris Minor. However, beyond these features there is little in common with the Minor.

The Wolseley 1500 and Riley 1.5 derivatives of the Morris Minor, which were produced between 1957 and 1965, featured similar 'chassis' and running gear to that used on the Minor. These two models had torsion-bar independent front suspension, which was like that used on the Minor - except that it was modified slightly and uprated for these heavier vehicles. The engines and gearboxes used in these models were different, the engine being the larger B-series unit.

As motoring journalists at the time noted, "the overall width" of these cars was "the same as the Minor" but they offered "more internal room, the centre pillars being set two inches farther apart." Wheelbase and track were identical to those of the Minor. However, although the overall width of the Wolseley/Riley was the same as the Morris Minor, the bodyshell (which they shared) was an entirely different design. Contrary to popular belief, the whole body structure of these models differs totally from the Minor body structure - as anyone who has restored a Riley or Wolseley will testify. The Minor underframe has a similar general layout, but is completely different in detail. As a reflection of the more recent design of the Wolseley and Riley and in order to achieve greater rigidity and less resonance in their

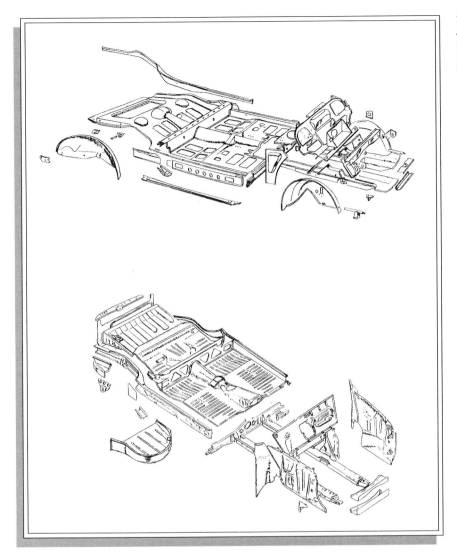

bodyshells, most of the inner structural panels carry greater amounts of swaged stiffening corrugations (or ridges). The panels tend to be made up of larger sections when compared with the Minor.

The Wolseley/Riley models were a more modern concept, originating in the Longbridge design office (Austin) and were nothing whatsoever to do with Issigonis or the Morris part of BMC. The Wolseley/Riley cars were styled by Dick Burzi, and not surprisingly reflected contemporary Austin thinking. As Jonathan Wood has commented, after the 1952 merger of Austin and Morris and the formation of the British Motor Corporation, it is noticeable that "Austin rather than Morris engineering policy dominated corporate thought."

A comparison of Riley 1.5 and Morris Minor underframe drawings clearly shows the differences between these two models.

Appendix II
Specification & performance of the Minor & its contemporaries

CARS OF THE EARLY 1950s					
	Minor (Series MM)	Ford Anglia	Triumph Mayflower	Austin A30	Renault 750 (4CV)
Weight (cwt)	15.3	15	18.8	14	12
Bhp	27	23.4	38	28	21
Max speed (mph)	62.3	57.2	65	63.6	59.5
0-50mph (seconds)	24.2	38.3	23.9	23.8	24.8
Mpg (overall)	40.5	36.2	33.5	38.6	43.2
1953 price*	£373	£313	£450	£355	£445
Overall length	12'5.5"	12'10"	13'0"	11'4.6"	11'10"
Overall width	5'0"	4'9"	5'2"	4'7.1"	4'8.3"
Front seat to roof distance	37"	37.5"	35"	37"	35"
Rear seat to roof distance	34"	35.5"	33"	35"	34"

Note: UK list price, excluding purchase tax. (Data compiled from Autocar and Motor sources).

CARS OF THE LATE 1960s				
	1968 price*	Maximum speed (mph)	0-60 (seconds)	MPG (overall)
Minor 1000 (2-dr saloon)	£476	73.4	24.8	34
Minor 1000 (4-dr saloon)	£501	73.4	24.8	34
Ford Escort (2-dr saloon)	£567	79	22.3	28
Vauxhall Viva (2-dr saloon)	£551	78	19.7	31
Morris 1100 (2-dr saloon)	£545	79	21.9	35
Morris Mini (2-dr saloon)	£438	71.8	29.7	42
Triumph Herald 1200 (2-dr saloon)	£524	77	25.8	29
Skoda 1000 MB (4-dr saloon)	£475	75	30.8	34
VW 1200 Beetle (2-dr saloon)	£515	71.7	27.5	33
Citroen Ami Tourisme (4-dr saloon)	£508	68	44	48
Fiat 1100R (4-dr saloon)	£554	73	28.6	30
Fiat 124 (4-dr saloon)	£640	83	15.9	28

*Note: UK list price, excluding purchase tax. (Data compiled from Autocar).

Appendix III
Sales data on the Minor & its contemporaries

PREWAR BRITISH-BUILT BESTSELLERS	
Morris Eight (1934-53)	394,000
Morris Oxford and Cowley (1913-35)	390,000
Austin Seven	300,000 (plus)
Model T Ford	300,000 (approx.)
Austin Ten (1932-47)	283,000
Ford Model Y	157,668

POSTWAR BRITISH-BUILT BESTSELLERS	
BMC Mini	5,065,220
Ford Cortina	4,279,079
BMC 1100/1300	2,132,980
Ford Escort (1968-80)	2,036,169
Morris Minor	1,619,857
Vauxhall Viva	1,597,063
Hillman Hunter/Paykan	1,486,643

POSTWAR BRITISH-BUILT BESTSELLERS (cont'd)	
Morris Marina/Ital	1,338,392
Ford Anglia 105E (1959)	1,083,955
Austin Cambridge/Morris Oxford (Farina)	864,000 (approx.)
Ford Anglia/Prefect/Popular (1953)	843,832
Hillman Avenger	832,804
Austin Allegro	667,192
Austin A40 (1947-56)	633,891
Triumph Herald	599,521
Ford Consul (1950-62)	581,481
Austin A30/A35	578,834
Ford (upright) Anglia and Prefect	537,913
Triumph 1300/Dolomite/Toledo	529,922
MGB	523,681

Please note - these figures were correct in December 1987. Sales for recent models such as the BL Metro, Ford Fiesta, Ford Sierra and Vauxhall Cavalier are not included. (Data compiled from Adeney, 1989).

ANNUAL SALES OF MORRIS MINOR CARS (1948-71)			
1948	1,215	1960	95,350*
1949	28,590	1961	60,800*
1950	48,061	1962	58,385*
1951	48,341	1963	45,900
1952	47,817	1964	41,385
1953	59,101	1965	39,008
1954	73,491	1966	38,610
1955	88,773	1967	37,922
1956	68,916	1968	31,640*
1957	103,944*	1969	28,275*
1958	115,000*	1970	20,102
1959	107,000*	1971	5,705

Figures marked with an asterisk * are approximate. (Data compiled from Skilleter, 1981).

The Secret Life of the Morris Minor

MORRIS MINOR TOTAL PRODUCTION FIGURES			
Model	Cars	Vans & pick-ups	Total
Series MM	176,002	0	176,002
Series II	269,838	48,513	318,351
1000 (948cc)	544,048	100,631	644,679
1000 (1098cc)	303,443	177,482	480,825
Total	**1,293,331**	**326,626**	**1,619,857**
(Data compiled from Skilleter, 1981).			

Appendix IV
Production changes
by year

DATE	PRODUCTION CHANGE OR INNOVATION
Sept. 48	First 2-door MM saloon produced.
April 49	New style, triangular-shaped rear stop tail light units fitted.
Oct. 49	Door surround/top painted instead of chrome.
1950	Two sun visors fitted as standard.
Oct. 50	4-door saloon available, with headlights fitted high up in the wings. Separate sidelights in revised grille panel. Other versions (2-door saloons and tourers) gradually shared these new features from early 1951 onwards.
1951	Split bumper and fillet discontinued. One piece valance and bumper blade introduced. Painted radiator grille introduced (chromium plated grille an optional extra). Over-riders fitted to 4-door saloon bumpers. Bonnet altered. Tourer given new hood of revised design and fixed rear side windows (to replace the removable sidescreens which had been used previously).
August 52	803cc ohv engine fitted in 4-door saloon (now called Series II).
Jan. 53	All models fitted with ohv engine.
May 53	Light commercial versions introduced.
Oct. 53	Traveller introduced. De luxe models for all versions of cars available, featuring heater, leather seats, over-riders and passenger sun visor.
1954	'A' type rear axle and standard swivel pin assembly introduced. Horizontal grille bars introduced. Separate instrument gauges replaced by single speedometer/instrument gauge. Open gloveboxes. Larger rear light fitting, incorporating reflector.
Oct. 56	803cc engined (Series II version) discontinued. New Minor '1000' version introduced. This featured a 948cc ohv engine, and a new one piece, curved windscreen and larger rear window. Dished steering wheel. Glovebox lids fitted. Deeper rear wings.
Dec. 56	New, strengthened steering swivel pin assembly fitted.
March 57	Fuel tank enlarged (taking 6 instead of 5 gallons).

The Secret Life of the Morris Minor

DATE	PRODUCTION CHANGE OR INNOVATION
1958	Courtesy light switches fitted in front doors. Rear springs changed from 7-leaf-type to 5-leaf-type.
Feb. 59	Dry paper air cleaner fitted.
1960	HS type SU carburettor fitted.
Jan. 61	350 Minor "Millions" produced in lilac colour paint with white upholstery and special badges.
Oct. 61	Semaphore type direction indicators discontinued. Flashing direction indicators incorporated into front and rear lamps. Glovebox lid removed. Seatbelt anchorage points built in to all models.
1962	948cc engine discontinued - new 1098cc engine fitted to Minor 1000s.
April 1963	Fresh air heater introduced.
Oct. 1963	Old (opposed) style windscreen wipers replaced by newer type working in tandem. Toughened windscreen introduced. New design combined side/flasher lamps at front and rear. Additional round, amber light fitted to rear of Traveller. New type air cleaner fitted.
Oct. 1964	New design facia panel. Glovebox on passenger side fitted with lid. Different trim and seating. Plastic rimmed interior mirror. Two spoke safety dished steering wheel. Fresh air heater performance improved. Combined ignition/starter switch.
Oct. 1966	Sealed beam headlamps fitted.
Oct. 1967	New type paper cleaner introduced.
June 1969	Convertible discontinued.
Late 1969	Oil filter switch ceased to be fitted. Amber warning lens fitted but not used.
1970	During the last months of production, some models were fitted with an alternator instead of a dynamo.
Nov. 1970	Saloon production discontinued.
1971	Last Travellers and commercial vehicles produced.

(Sources: Newell,1982; Newell, 1984; Skilleter, 1981).

Glossary

&

Bibliography

Abbreviations
bhp .... Brake horsepower
BMC .... British Motor Corporation
cc .... Cubic centimetre
LCV .... Light Commercial Vehicle
mpg .... Miles per gallon
mph .... Miles per hour
ohc .... Overhead camshaft
ohv .... Overhead valves

Car terms
Aerodynamics .... study of the motion of solid bodies through the air.
Alternator .... engine-driven electric generator which produces an alternating current.
Axle tramp .... Alternate winding-up and unwinding of a Hotchkiss drive axle on its leaf springs under fierce acceleration; more likely on rough or loose surfaces which cause the wheels to lose traction and thus allow the springs to unwind.
Beam axle .... rigid transverse member carrying front wheels that do not have independent suspension.
Bottom-end .... colloquial term for the crankshaft, its main bearings, and the connecting rod big-end bearings.
Coil spring .... helix of spring steel rod or wire, which is twisted when the spring is compressed or extended.
Corrosion .... oxidation of a metal through attack by damp, acid or other chemicals.

The Secret Life of the Morris Minor

Dynamo .... direct-current generator.

Fastback .... body in which the roof line runs in an uninterrupted sweep to the tail of the car and embodies a rear window at a considerable angle to the vertical.

Front-wheel-drive .... type of transmission system in which the engine drives the front wheels.

Grille .... decorative grid on the front of a car.

Handling .... the steering and cornering characteristics of a car, particularly when it is driven hard.

Horizontally opposed engine .... engine with an equal number of cylinders horizontal on each side of the crankshaft.

Horsepower tax .... (see RAC rating).

Hotchkiss drive .... Rear suspension in which semi-elliptic road springs absorb the driving torque reaction.

Independent suspension .... suspension system in which each wheel has its own linkage to the vehicle body or chassis and its own spring, allowing it to move without influencing another wheel.

Leaf spring .... suspension spring built up from a series of steel strips, or leaves.

Live rear axle .... beam type axle containing the crownwheel and pinion, differential gears and halfshafts.

Master cylinder .... first stage of a hydraulic clutch or brake system; operation of the pedal causes the piston in the master cylinder to move, thus developing hydraulic pressure in the pipelines and flexible tubing leading to the clutch or brake operating cylinders.

Overhead valve engine .... engine in which the valves are in the cylinder head above the combustion chambers.

Rack and pinion .... type of steering unit in which a pinion at the bottom of the steering column engages a straight rack that moves sideways in relation to the car as the pinion is turned. The ends of the rack are connected to the steering arms by short, jointed links.

RAC rating .... (horsepower tax) - early taxation formula based on
.... estimated horsepower (the number of cylinders mul-
.... tiplied by the square of the bore in inches, divided by
.... 2.5, the stroke being disregarded).

Semi-automatic transmission .... transmission system in which the clutch functions are performed automatically, but the driver still has to select the various gears manually.

Semi-elliptic spring ...... leaf spring in the shape of a half ellipse often formed of narrow strips of spring steel.

Sidevalve engine .... engine in which the inlet and exhaust valves are along side the cylinder, not in the cylinder head (power out put and fuel economy are inferior to those of an overhead valve engine).

Steering box .... mechanical device at the lower end of the steering column; it transmits the rotation of the steering wheel to the steering linkage controlling the position of the front wheels.

Steering column .... metal shaft that carries the steering wheel at its upper end and which is connected to the steering box at the other end.

Swing-axles .... driveshafts connected to the final drive by universal joints, but rigidly connected to the wheels at their outer ends.

Swivel pin .... a steel forging carrying the front wheel assembly.

Torque .... turning effort exerted by or on a moving part. In the case of an engine it is the mean turning effort exerted on the crankshaft by the pistons and is available for propelling the car. Maximum torque is usually produced at half to two-thirds of the speed at which the engine develops its maximum power.

Toughened glass
windscreen .... single-sheet safety glass windscreen specially heat treated so that, if broken, it separates into granules which do not cause injury.

Transverse leaf spring .. semi-elliptic spring (qv.) mounted in an inverted position on the chassis with its free ends shackled to the axle.

Torsion bar .... steel bar used in some suspension systems instead of a spring. The bar is fixed at one end and twisted at the other by a lever attached to the suspension linkage.

Trunnion .... member in some independent front suspension systems for connecting the lower wishbone with the steering swivel.

Unitary construction .... body structure that has no separate chassis. The body itself forms the load bearing structure of the vehicle.

Wishbones .... pivoted, triangle-shaped links that connect each wheel in an independent suspension system to the car's body.

Bibliography

Primary sources (sales brochures, workshop manuals, etc.)

BMC, (1967) *Morris Can Take It* sales brochure.
BMC, *Morris Minor 1000 Parts List*, No. AKD3542, Nuffield Press.
BMC, *Morris Minor Workshop Manual* Issue 5, No. AKD530E, Nuffield Press.
BMC, (1963) Morris 6 Cwt Van And Pick-Up sales brochure, Nuffield Press.
BMC, *Riley One-Point-Five Parts List*, No. AKD759, Nuffield Press.
British Leyland, (1969) Morris Minor 1000 sales brochure, Nuffield Press.
British Leyland, (1971) Morris Minor 1000 Traveller sales brochure, Nuffield Press.
Morris Motors, (1950) Minor, Oxford, Six sales brochure, Nuffield Press.
Morris Motors, (1947) Morris Eight Series E sales brochures, Nuffield Press.
Morris Motors, (1952) Morris Minor 4-Door Saloon sales brochure, Nuffield Press.
Morris Motors (1953) Quality First sales brochure, Nuffield Press.
Morris Motors, (July 1949) *The New Morris Cars*, Nuffield Press.
Nuffield Organisation, (February 1950) *A Great Industrial Achievement*, Nuffield Press.

Nuffield Organisation, (August 1952) *A New Car Is Born*, Nuffield Press.
Nuffield Organisation, (1949) *The Nuffield Exhibits*, Nuffield Press.

Journals and periodicals
Autocar.
Autoclassic.
Auto Express.
Automobile Engineer.
Classic American.
Classic and Sportscar.
Collector's Car.
Country Life.
Independent.
Minor Matters (The Magazine of the Morris Minor Owners Club).
Motor.
Motoring.
MotorSport.
Motor Trend.
Oxford Mail.
Sunday Mail.
Thoroughbred and Classic Cars.
Your Classic.

Secondary sources (includes collections of primary sources)
Adeney, M. (1989) *The Motor Makers: the turbulent history of Britain's car industry*, Fontana.
Aldcroft, D. (1974) *Studies In British Transport History 1870-1970*, David & Charles.
Allen, M. (1985) *British Family Cars of the Fifties*, Haynes.
Allen, M. (1989) *British Family Cars of the Early Sixties*, Haynes.
Andrews, P. and Brunner, E. (1955) *The Life Of Lord Nuffield: a study in enterprise and benevolence*, Basil Blackwell, Oxford.
Angelucci, E. and Bellucci, A. (1975) *The Automobile*, Macdonald, London.
Armi, C.E. (1988) *The Art Of American Car Design*, Pennsylvania State University Press.
Autocar, (1984) *Morris Minor* (compiled from the archives of *Autocar*), Temple Press.
Automobile Association, (1985) *The A.A. Book of the Car*, Drive Publications.
Ayres, Pam. (1978) *Thoughts of a Late-Night Knitter*, Arrow Books.
Bagwell, P. (1974) *The Transport Revolution From 1770*, Batsford, London.
Barker, R. and Harding, A. (eds.) (1970) *Automobile Design: great designers and their work*, David & Charles.
Barker, T. and Savage, C. (1974) *An Economic History Of Transport In Britain* (3rd edn), Hutchinson University Library, London.
Barnett, C. (1988) *The Audit Of War*, Papermac.
British Coal, (1990) *A Guide To Steam Trains In The British Isles*.
Broad, R. (1975) *Citroen*, William Luscombe Publishing.
Brunt, A. (1983) *Phaidon Guide To Furniture* (2nd edn), Phaidon, Oxford.
Clarke, R. (ed.) *Morris Minor Collection No. 1* (1948-80 road tests etc), Brooklands Books.
Davies, W. (1973) *Diesel Rail Traction*, Almark Publishing, London.
Edwards, H. (1983) *The Morris Motor Car 1913-1983*, Moorland Publishing.
Halsey, A.H. (ed.) (1972) *Trends In British Society Since 1900*, Macmillan.
Hebdige, D. (1989) *Hiding In The Light*, Routledge, London.
Heskett, J. (1980) *Industrial Design*, Thames & Hudson.
Hessayon, Dr D.G. (1983) *The Tree And Shrub Expert*, PBI Publications.
Hillier, B. (1975) *Austerity Binge: the decorative arts of the Forties and Fifties*, Studio Vista, London.

Hillier, B. (1983) *The Style of the Century 1900-1980*, Herbert Press, London.

Holdsworth, A. (1988) *Out Of The Dolls House: the story of women in the twentieth century*, BBC Books.

Lacey, R. (1986) *Ford The Men And The Machine*, Heinemann.

Lowe, P. and Goyder, J. (1983) *Environmental Groups In Politics*, George Allen & Unwin, London.

Lucie-Smith, E. (1983) *A History Of Industrial Design*, Phaidon, Oxford.

MacCarthy, F. *A History of British Design 1830-1970*, (1970) George Allen & Unwin.

Marwick, A. (1990) *British Society Since 1945*, Penguin.

Mclellan, J. (1975) *Bodies Beautiful: a history of car styling and craftsmanship*, David & Charles.

Morris Minor Centre, (1982) *The Morris Minor Centre Catalogue*, Morris Minor Centre Publishing, Bath.

Morris Minor Centre, (1988) *The Morris Minor Centre 1976- 1987*, Morris Minor Centre Publishing, Bath.

Motor and Thoroughbred and Classic Cars On Morris Minor 1948-1983 (compiled from *Motor* and *Thoroughbred And Classic Cars* archives) Brooklands Books.

Munby, D. (1978) *Inland Transport Statistics Great Britain 1900-1970* Volume 1, Clarendon Press, Oxford.

Nahum, A. (1988) *Alec Issigonis*, Design Council.

Newell, R. (1982) *Morris Minor and 1000 Super Profile*, Haynes.

Newell, R. (1984) *Morris Minor Series MM Super Profile*, Haynes.

Nicholson, M. (1970) *The Environmental Revolution: a guide for the new masters of the world*, Hodder & Stoughton, London.

Nicholson, M. (1990) *The New Environmental Age*, Cambridge University Press.

Olyslager, P. (ed.) (1972) *American Cars of the 1940s*, Frederick Warne & Co. (Note - more recent editions edited by B. Vanderveen).

Overy, R. (1976) *William Morris, Viscount Nuffield*, Europa Publications Ltd.

Plowden, W. (1971) *The Motor Car And Politics*, Bodley Head.

Practical Classics, Practical Classics on Morris Minor Restoration, Brooklands Books.

Rhys, D. (1972) *The Motor Industry: an economic survey*, Butterworths.

Robson, G. (1987) *The Cars Of BMC*, Motor Racing Publications.

Samuel, R. (ed.) (1985) *Making Cars: a history of car making in Cowley*, Routledge & Kegan Paul.

Sedgwick, M. (1979) *The Motor Car 1946-56*, Batsford, London.

Sedgwick, M. (1979) *Cars of the Thirties and Forties*, Hamlyn.

Sedgwick, M. (1983) *Cars of the Fifties and Sixties*, Temple Press.

Skilleter, P. (1981) *Morris Minor: the world's supreme small car*, Osprey.

Skilleter, P. (1989) *Morris Minor: the world's supreme small car* (3rd edn), Osprey.

Society of Motor Manufacturers and Traders, (1948) *Motor Exhibition Catalogue : Oct-Nov 1948*, Doulton Press.

Society of Motor Manufacturers and Traders, (August 1990) *The Motor Vehicle and the Environment*.

Sparke, P. (1986) *An Introduction To Design And Culture In The Twentieth Century*, Allen & Unwin, London.

Sparke, P. (1987) *Design In Context*, Bloomsbury Publishing.

Speed, J. (ed.) (1952) *British Motor Cars*, Foulis & Co., London.

Thomas, Sir Miles. (1964) *Out On A Wing: an autobiography*, Michael Joseph, London.

Turner, G. (1963) *The Car Makers*, Eyre & Spottiswoode.

Turner, G. (1973) *The Leyland Papers*, Pan Books.

Vanderveen, B. (ed.) (1986) *British Cars of the Late Forties 1947-1949*, Haynes.

Ward, I. (1981) *Motoring For The Millions*, Blandford Press.

Wood, J. (1988) *Wheels Of Misfortune: the rise and fall of the British motor industry*, Sidgwick & Jackson.

Young, P. (1987) *The Himalayan Minor*, Speedwell Books.

Index

The Secret Life of the Morris Minor